GOODSON MUMBA

Mental Health Matters

Cultivating Wellbeing in the Workplace

Contents

Preface

In the ever-evolving landscape of the modern workplace, mental health has emerged as a pivotal concern that influences not only the well-being of individuals but also the overall success and sustainability of organizations. The recognition that mental health matters is no longer just a moral imperative— it is a strategic necessity.

This book, "Mental Health Matters: Cultivating Wellbeing in the Workplace," is born out of a deep-seated conviction that the mental health of employees should be at the forefront of organizational priorities. Over the past decade, we have witnessed a significant shift in the way businesses perceive and address mental health. Yet, despite the progress, there remains a critical need for comprehensive guidance on fostering a culture of wellbeing that is both effective and sustainable.

As professionals who have spent years working at the intersection of mental health and organizational development, we have seen firsthand the profound impact that a supportive and inclusive workplace can have on an individual's mental health. We have also witnessed the detrimental effects that a lack of attention to mental health can have on productivity, morale, and overall organizational health.

This book is designed to be a practical guide for leaders, managers, and employees alike. It provides actionable insights and strategies for creating a workplace environment where mental health is prioritized, and where employees feel valued and supported. Each chapter delves into critical aspects of mental health in the workplace, offering a blend of theoretical foundations, real-world examples, and practical tools.

In Chapter 1, we begin with a foundational understanding of mental health in the workplace, exploring its importance and the common challenges faced. We then move on to discuss the impact of mental health on productivity and morale, the stigma that still surrounds mental health at work, and the crucial role of organizational culture in supporting mental wellbeing.

Subsequent chapters provide a roadmap for building a foundation of support, addressing stress management, building resilience, and fostering social connections. We explore the role of leadership in promoting mental health and the importance of creating psychological safety. We also provide guidance on supporting employees with mental health conditions and integrating mental health into company policies, benefits, and programs.

By the end of this book, we hope you will be equipped with the knowledge and tools necessary to cultivate a culture of wellbeing within your organization. Our goal is to inspire a transformative shift in how mental health is perceived and addressed in the workplace, fostering environments where every individual can thrive.

Mental health matters. It matters to the individuals who make up the fabric of our organizations, and it matters to the organizations themselves. By prioritizing mental health, we can create workplaces that are not only more compassionate and inclusive but also more innovative, productive, and resilient.

We invite you to join us on this journey toward cultivating wellbeing in the workplace, and we are excited to share the

insights and strategies that can help make this vision a reality.
With gratitude and optimism,
Goodson Mumba

Acknowledgement

I would like to eternally and gratefully acknowledge the Almighty God for the infinite intelligence from His universal mind where we draw from all that we come to know and are yet to know. May I also acknowledge and thank everyone that has played a part in my journey of life in terms of spiritual, moral, emotional and material support.

Dedication

I extend my sincerest gratitude to my beloved wife, Edith Mumba, and our children, Angelina, Lubuto, Letticia, Lulumbi, and Butusho, for their unwavering support and understanding throughout the conception, writing, and eventual publication of this book, despite the sacrifices and challenges they endured.

Disclaimer

ix

This book is a work of fiction. Names, characters, businesses, places, events, and incidents are either the products of the author's imagination or used in a fictitious manner. Any resemblance to actual persons, living or dead, or actual events is purely coincidental.

1

Chapter 1: Understanding Mental Health in the Workplace

The importance of mental health awareness

"Breaking the Silence: Recognizing the Invisible Struggle"

The fluorescent lights flickered overhead, casting a sterile glow over the bustling office floor. Sarah sat at her desk, eyes fixed on the computer screen, but her mind was elsewhere. The mounting pressure of deadlines and client demands weighed heavily on her shoulders, a constant presence she couldn't shake.

As Sarah glanced around the office, she couldn't help but notice the subtle signs of strain etched on her coworkers' faces. The once vibrant atmosphere now felt tinged with tension, like a pressure cooker on the verge of boiling over.

One morning, as Sarah sipped her lukewarm coffee, a hushed whisper rippled through the office. Alex, the usually cheerful graphic designer, had called in sick for the third day in a row.

Concerned murmurs filled the air as colleagues exchanged worried glances.

Sarah's heart sank as she recalled the last time she had seen Alex. He had seemed distant, his usually bright eyes clouded with exhaustion. But like so many others, Sarah had brushed aside her concerns, chalking it up to the stresses of the job.

As the day wore on, Sarah couldn't shake the nagging feeling that something was deeply wrong. She couldn't ignore the sinking realization that mental health was an issue lurking in the shadows of their busy workplace, waiting to be acknowledged.

That evening, Sarah sat alone in her apartment, the silence punctuated only by the soft glow of her laptop screen. With a determined furrow of her brow, she began to research the importance of mental health awareness in the workplace.

As she delved deeper into articles and studies, Sarah's eyes widened with understanding. She learned that mental health awareness wasn't just about acknowledging the existence of conditions like anxiety and depression—it was about recognizing the human cost of ignoring them.

With a newfound sense of purpose burning in her chest, Sarah closed her laptop. She knew that she couldn't stay silent any longer. The time had come to shine a light on the invisible struggles of her colleagues and advocate for change in their workplace culture. And so, armed with knowledge and determination, Sarah embarked on her journey to make mental health matter in their office.

Common mental health challenges in the workplace

"Unveiling the Shadows: Confronting Workplace Mental Health Challenges"

The next day at the office, Sarah's mind buzzed with newfound awareness as she observed her surroundings with a fresh perspective. The hum of keyboards and the distant chatter of phone calls seemed to take on a new significance, each sound a reminder of the silent struggles that lurked beneath the surface.

As Sarah made her rounds, she couldn't help but notice the telltale signs of stress etched into the faces of her colleagues. Michelle, the ever-efficient project manager, seemed unusually frazzled, her normally composed demeanor faltering under the weight of looming deadlines.

Nearby, David, a seasoned account executive, sat slumped at his desk, his usually vibrant energy replaced by a palpable sense of exhaustion. Sarah recalled the days when David had been the life of the office, his infectious laughter echoing through the halls. Now, his laughter was replaced by weary sighs, a stark reminder of the toll that relentless pressure could take.

With a heavy heart, Sarah realized that these were not isolated incidents—far from it. These were the faces of her coworkers, each one silently grappling with their own mental health challenges in the relentless pursuit of success.

As the day wore on, Sarah couldn't shake the gnawing feeling that she was witnessing a collective struggle, a silent epidemic that had infiltrated every corner of their workplace. From the interns to the executives, no one was immune to the insidious grip of stress, anxiety, and burnout.

With each passing hour, Sarah felt a growing sense of urgency. She knew that she couldn't stand idly by while her colleagues suffered in silence. It was time to confront the harsh realities of workplace mental health head-on and advocate for change.

That evening, as Sarah reflected on the events of the day, a steely resolve settled over her. Armed with empathy and determination, she vowed to be a voice for those who felt unheard, to shine a light on the shadows that had long plagued their workplace, and to pave the way for a future where mental health mattered as much as the bottom line.

Impact of mental health on productivity and morale

"The Silent Toll: Mental Health's Whisper in Productivity's Ear"

The following morning, Sarah arrived at the office with a renewed sense of purpose, her mind buzzing with the weight of her newfound mission. As she settled into her desk, she couldn't shake the sense of urgency that pulsed through her veins like a drumbeat.

Throughout the day, Sarah couldn't help but notice the ripple effects of unchecked mental health struggles on productivity and morale. Meetings that once crackled with energy now felt sluggish, each minute ticking by like an eternity as distracted minds struggled to focus.

Emails went unanswered, deadlines slipped, and tension hung thick in the air like a suffocating fog. The vibrant buzz of creativity that had once permeated the office seemed to have dulled, replaced by a sense of resignation and fatigue.

Sarah watched as her colleagues pushed themselves to the brink, their once-sharp minds now dulled by the weight of stress and anxiety. It was a sobering reminder of the toll that unchecked mental health issues could take on even the most talented and dedicated professionals.

As the day wore on, Sarah couldn't help but feel a sense of frustration building within her. She knew that their workplace was capable of so much more—that beneath the surface of exhaustion and burnout lay a wellspring of untapped potential, waiting to be unleashed.

With a determined glint in her eye, Sarah vowed to make a change. She knew that by prioritizing mental health and wellbeing in their workplace, they could not only unlock greater productivity and innovation but also cultivate a culture of resilience and support that would benefit everyone.

That evening, as Sarah gathered her thoughts and prepared to leave the office, she couldn't shake the feeling that she was standing at the precipice of something momentous. Armed with the knowledge of the impact of mental health on productivity and morale, she was ready to lead the charge toward a brighter, more compassionate future for their workplace.

Stigma surrounding mental health at work

"Breaking the Chains: Shattering the Stigma of Silence"

As Sarah entered the office the next day, a sense of determination burned bright within her. Today, she would confront one of the most pervasive barriers to workplace mental health: the suffocating cloak of stigma that shrouded the topic in silence.

As Sarah navigated the familiar maze of cubicles, she couldn't help but feel the weight of the unspoken taboo that hung heavy in the air. Mental health was whispered about in hushed tones, if it was acknowledged at all, relegated to the shadows of polite conversation.

She observed the subtle glances exchanged between colleagues when the topic of stress or anxiety arose, the uncomfortable shifting of chairs and forced smiles that masked deeper discomfort. It was as if mental health had become the elephant in the room, too unwieldy and intimidating to address head-on.

Sarah knew that this culture of silence only served to perpetuate the stigma surrounding mental health, pushing those in need further into the shadows and preventing meaningful dialogue and support from taking root.

Determined to break the chains of stigma that bound their workplace, Sarah decided to take action. With a steady voice and unwavering resolve, she called for an impromptu meeting in the breakroom, inviting her colleagues to join her in a candid conversation about mental health.

As the room filled with hesitant faces and nervous murmurs, Sarah took a deep breath and began to speak. She shared her own struggles with stress and anxiety, laying bare the vulnerabilities that had long been hidden beneath a facade of strength and professionalism.

To her surprise, instead of judgment or rejection, Sarah was met with a wave of empathy and understanding. Her colleagues shared their own experiences, their voices growing stronger with each word as the walls of stigma crumbled around them.

By the end of the meeting, Sarah could feel a shift in the air—a sense of liberation and empowerment that had been absent before. Together, they had shattered the stigma of silence that had held them captive for so long, paving the way for a future where mental health was met with compassion and support, rather than judgment and shame.

As Sarah left the breakroom that day, a renewed sense of hope burned bright within her. Armed with the knowledge that they were stronger together, she knew that they could overcome any challenge that lay ahead, united in their commitment to prioritizing mental health in their workplace.

Legal and ethical considerations in addressing workplace mental health

"Navigating the Gray: Ethics and Laws in the Mental Health Landscape"

As Sarah stepped into the office on a crisp morning, the weight of responsibility settled upon her shoulders like a heavy cloak. Today, she would confront the intricate web of legal and ethical considerations that loomed over the landscape of workplace mental health.

With each passing day, Sarah had become acutely aware of the delicate balance between providing support for mental health in the workplace and respecting the boundaries of privacy and autonomy. It was a tightrope walk fraught with uncertainty, where missteps could have far-reaching consequences.

As she settled into her desk, Sarah's thoughts turned to the legal and ethical framework that governed their workplace. She knew that while their intentions were noble, they must navigate this complex terrain with care and diligence.

Throughout the day, Sarah found herself poring over legal documents and ethics guidelines, her brow furrowed in concentration as she sought to unravel the intricacies of their obligations as employers and colleagues.

She learned of the importance of confidentiality and discretion when it came to handling sensitive information about an employee's mental health, understanding that trust was the foundation upon which any meaningful support must be built.

She also discovered the legal protections afforded to individuals with mental health conditions under the Americans with Disabilities Act (ADA), recognizing the importance of providing reasonable accommodations and ensuring equal treatment in the workplace.

But amidst the sea of legalese and ethical quandaries, Sarah found a glimmer of hope—a beacon of light that cut through the darkness of uncertainty. She realized that while the path ahead might be fraught with challenges, it was also paved with opportunity—the opportunity to foster a workplace culture that prioritized compassion, understanding, and support for all.

Armed with this newfound knowledge, Sarah resolved to forge ahead, guided by the principles of fairness and integrity. She knew that by navigating the gray areas of ethics and laws with care and compassion, they could create a workplace where mental health mattered—not just as a legal obligation, but as a fundamental human right.

The role of organizational culture in supporting mental wellbeing

"Cultivating Compassion: Nurturing Mental Wellbeing in Organizational Soil"

As Sarah stepped into the bustling office, a sense of anticipation tingled in the air. Today, she would delve into the vital role of organizational culture in nurturing mental wellbeing—a journey that would shape the very fabric of their workplace.

With each passing day, Sarah had come to realize that their workplace was more than just a collection of desks and computers—it was a living, breathing ecosystem, shaped by the values, beliefs, and behaviors of its inhabitants.

As she observed her colleagues bustling about, she couldn't help but marvel at the subtle nuances that defined their organizational culture. From the way they greeted each other in the morning to the rituals they observed during meetings, every interaction was a reflection of the collective mindset that governed their workplace.

But Sarah knew that beneath the surface lay a deeper truth—one that spoke to the heart of their ability to support mental wellbeing. She knew that organizational culture wasn't just about superficial rituals or catchy slogans—it was about creating an environment where employees felt valued, respected, and supported in every aspect of their lives.

Throughout the day, Sarah engaged her colleagues in conversations about the importance of organizational culture in fostering mental wellbeing. Together, they explored the ways in which their workplace culture could be reshaped to prioritize compassion, empathy, and inclusivity.

They discussed the power of small gestures, like offering words of encouragement or taking the time to check in on a struggling coworker. They brainstormed ways to promote work-life balance, whether through flexible schedules or remote work options. And they reflected on the importance of fostering a sense of belonging and community, where every voice was heard and every perspective valued.

As the day drew to a close, Sarah couldn't help but feel a sense of optimism bubbling within her. She knew that by nurturing a culture of compassion and support, they could create a workplace where mental wellbeing thrived—a place where employees felt empowered to bring their whole selves to work, knowing that they would be met with understanding and acceptance.

Armed with this newfound understanding, Sarah resolved to be a catalyst for change in their organizational culture, leading by example and inspiring others to join her in the journey toward a brighter, more compassionate future.

2

Chapter 2: Building a Foundation of Support

Establishing mental health policies and procedures

"Laying the Groundwork: Building a Fortress of Support"

As Sarah entered the office on a crisp Monday morning, a sense of purpose pulsed through her veins like a steady heartbeat. Today marked the beginning of a new chapter—a chapter dedicated to building a foundation of support for mental wellbeing in their workplace.

With a determined stride, Sarah made her way to the conference room, where she was scheduled to meet with the executive team to discuss the establishment of mental health policies and procedures.

As she took her seat at the head of the table, Sarah felt a swell of nervous anticipation rise within her. She knew that the decisions made in this room would lay the groundwork for a future where mental health was prioritized and supported at every level of the organization.

With a steady voice, Sarah began to outline her vision for the company's mental health policies and procedures. She emphasized the importance of creating a framework that provided clear guidelines and resources for employees seeking support, while also safeguarding their privacy and autonomy.

Together, they discussed the need for comprehensive training programs to educate managers and employees about mental health awareness, destigmatization, and how to recognize and respond to signs of distress in their colleagues.

They explored the idea of implementing a confidential support system, where employees could access counseling services and resources without fear of judgment or reprisal. And they brainstormed ways to integrate mental health into existing HR policies and benefits, ensuring that every aspect of the employee experience was designed with their wellbeing in mind.

As the meeting drew to a close, Sarah couldn't help but feel a sense of pride wash over her. She knew that the road ahead would be challenging, but she also knew that they were taking a crucial first step toward creating a workplace where mental health mattered—a workplace where every employee felt supported, valued, and empowered to thrive.

Armed with the commitment of her colleagues and the strength of their collective vision, Sarah left the conference room with a renewed sense of purpose. Together, they would build a fortress of support—one brick at a time, until it stood as a beacon of hope and compassion in their workplace and beyond.

Training managers and employees on mental health awareness

"Empowering Minds: Illuminating the Path to Awareness"

As the sun rose over the city skyline, casting golden hues across the office windows, Sarah stood at the front of the conference room, ready to embark on the next phase of their journey toward mental health support.

With a click of her presentation remote, Sarah illuminated the screen with a series of slides outlining the importance of mental health awareness training for managers and employees alike.

She spoke passionately about the need to destigmatize mental health in the workplace, to create an environment where open dialogue and understanding flourished.

As she delved into the specifics of the training program, Sarah's voice filled with conviction. She outlined the curriculum, which would cover topics ranging from common mental health disorders to strategies for providing support to colleagues in distress.

She emphasized the role that managers played as frontline advocates for mental health, their ability to recognize signs of struggle in their team members and provide the necessary support and resources.

But Sarah didn't stop there. She also underscored the importance of empowering all employees to play a role in fostering a culture of mental health awareness and support. She spoke of the power of empathy and active listening, of the small gestures that could make a world of difference to someone in need.

As the training session unfolded, Sarah watched with pride as her colleagues engaged with the material, their eyes alight with understanding and empathy. She knew that this was more than just a training session—it was a catalyst for change, a spark that would ignite a revolution of compassion and support in their workplace.

As the session drew to a close, Sarah felt a swell of hope rise within her. She knew that with each mind they enlightened, each heart they opened, they were one step closer to creating a workplace where mental health was not just acknowledged, but embraced—a workplace where every employee felt seen, heard, and supported on their journey to wellbeing.

Creating a supportive and inclusive work environment

"Harmony in Diversity: Building a Tapestry of Support"

As the clock struck noon, Sarah gathered her thoughts and took a deep breath. It was time to delve into the heart of their mission—to create a workplace that embraced diversity and nurtured a sense of belonging for all.

With a sense of purpose burning bright within her, Sarah addressed her colleagues, her voice steady and resolute. She spoke of the importance of creating a workplace where every individual felt valued, respected, and included—a place where differences were not just tolerated, but celebrated.

She outlined their plan to foster a culture of support and inclusivity, where employees from all walks of life felt empowered to bring their authentic selves to work each day. She spoke of the need to cultivate empathy and understanding, to recognize and honor the unique experiences and perspectives that each person brought to the table.

As Sarah painted a vision of a workplace where diversity was not just a buzzword, but a guiding principle, she could feel the energy in the room shift. She saw nods of agreement and heard murmurs of approval as her colleagues embraced the idea of building a tapestry of support that reflected the rich diversity of their team.

Together, they brainstormed ways to promote inclusivity in their day-to-day interactions, whether through language and communication practices or through the creation of affinity groups and support networks for underrepresented employees.

They discussed the importance of providing resources and accommodations for employees with disabilities, ensuring that every individual had the tools they needed to thrive in their role. And they explored ways to address unconscious bias and discrimination in the workplace, fostering a culture where all employees felt safe and supported.

As the meeting drew to a close, Sarah felt a sense of pride swell within her. She knew that building a supportive and inclusive work environment would not happen overnight, but she also knew that they were taking the first crucial steps toward creating a workplace where every individual felt valued, respected, and empowered to reach their full potential.

Armed with the commitment of her colleagues and the strength of their collective vision, Sarah left the conference room with a renewed sense of purpose. Together, they would build a workplace where harmony thrived—a place where diversity was not just accepted, but celebrated, and where every employee felt seen, heard, and supported on their journey to success.

Providing access to mental health resources and services

"Bridging the Gap: A Pathway to Mental Wellness"

As the afternoon sun cast warm rays through the office windows, Sarah stood before her colleagues, ready to tackle the next critical aspect of their mission—to provide access to mental health resources and services for all.

With a sense of urgency in her voice, Sarah outlined their plan to bridge the gap between need and support, ensuring that every employee had access to the resources and services they needed to prioritize their mental wellness.

She spoke of their commitment to providing comprehensive mental health benefits, including access to therapy, counseling, and psychiatric services. She emphasized the importance of removing barriers to care, whether through streamlined referral processes, telehealth options, or coverage for mental health medications.

As Sarah delved into the specifics of their plan, she could feel the weight of responsibility settle upon her shoulders. She knew that providing access to mental health resources was not just about ticking boxes—it was about saving lives, about offering hope and healing to those who needed it most.

Together, they brainstormed ways to raise awareness about the mental health resources available to employees, whether through informational sessions, email newsletters, or intranet portals. They discussed the importance of destigmatizing help-seeking behavior, encouraging employees to reach out for support without fear of judgment or reprisal.

They also explored the role of peer support networks and employee assistance programs (EAPs) in providing immediate support to those in crisis, ensuring that no one had to face their struggles alone.

As the meeting drew to a close, Sarah felt a sense of pride swell within her. She knew that by providing access to mental health resources and services, they were not just fulfilling a duty to their employees—they were offering a lifeline, a beacon of hope in the darkness of despair.

Armed with the commitment of her colleagues and the strength of their collective vision, Sarah left the conference room with a renewed sense of purpose. Together, they would build a pathway to mental wellness—a pathway lined with compassion, support, and the unwavering belief that every employee deserved the chance to thrive.

Implementing confidential support systems

"Shelter in the Storm: Building Confidential Sanctuaries"

As dusk settled over the city, bathing the office in a soft, golden glow, Sarah gathered her colleagues once more, ready to embark on the next phase of their journey—to implement confidential support systems that would serve as sanctuaries for those in need.

With a quiet resolve in her voice, Sarah outlined their plan to create confidential support systems that would provide a safe haven for employees to seek help and guidance in times of need.

She spoke of their commitment to confidentiality, emphasizing that every employee could trust that their struggles would be met with compassion and discretion. She detailed the various channels through which employees could access support, whether through dedicated helplines, online chat services, or in-person counseling sessions.

As Sarah painted a vision of these confidential support systems, she could feel the tension in the room ease, replaced by a sense of relief and reassurance. She saw nods of agreement and heard murmurs of approval as her colleagues embraced the idea of providing a lifeline for those who felt lost in the storm.

Together, they brainstormed ways to raise awareness about these support systems, ensuring that every employee knew how to access help when they needed it most. They discussed the importance of training managers and HR personnel to respond effectively to mental health crises, providing a compassionate and supportive response to those in distress.

They also explored the role of peer support networks in providing immediate support to those in crisis, offering a listening ear and a shoulder to lean on in times of need.

As the meeting drew to a close, Sarah felt a sense of gratitude wash over her. She knew that by implementing confidential support systems, they were not just offering a service—they were offering hope, a beacon of light in the darkness for those who felt lost and alone.

Armed with the commitment of her colleagues and the strength of their collective vision, Sarah left the conference room with a renewed sense of purpose. Together, they would build sanctuaries of support—places where every employee could find shelter in the storm, knowing that they were not alone on their journey to healing and wholeness.

Encouraging Open communication and destigmatization

"Breaking the Silence: Fostering a Culture of Openness"

As twilight descended upon the city, Sarah stood before her colleagues once more, the weight of their mission heavy upon her shoulders. Tonight, they would confront one of the most formidable barriers to mental health support—the stigma surrounding mental illness—and pave the way for a future where open communication and destigmatization reigned.

With a determined fire in her eyes, Sarah spoke of the need to break the silence surrounding mental health, to shatter the stigma that had kept so many silent and suffering in the shadows.

She shared her own struggles with anxiety and depression, laying bare the vulnerabilities that had long been hidden beneath a facade of strength and professionalism. She spoke of the fear and shame that had held her captive, the relentless whispers of doubt and self-judgment that had threatened to consume her.

But Sarah didn't stop there. She also spoke of the power of open communication, of the healing that could come from sharing our struggles with others and knowing that we were not alone. She encouraged her colleagues to speak up, to share their own stories and experiences, and to listen with empathy and understanding to those of others.

As she spoke, Sarah could feel the tension in the room begin to melt away, replaced by a sense of connection and solidarity. She saw tears in the eyes of her colleagues, heard the tremble in their voices as they shared their own stories of struggle and triumph.

Together, they brainstormed ways to foster open communication and destigmatization in their workplace, whether through lunchtime seminars, employee resource groups, or company-wide campaigns. They discussed the importance of language and messaging, ensuring that their words reflected compassion and understanding rather than judgment and stigma.

As the meeting drew to a close, Sarah felt a sense of hope swell within her. She knew that by encouraging open communication and destigmatization, they were not just changing the conversation—they were changing lives, offering a lifeline to those who had felt lost and alone for far too long.

Armed with the commitment of her colleagues and the strength of their collective vision, Sarah left the conference room with a renewed sense of purpose. Together, they would break the silence, shatter the stigma, and pave the way for a future where mental health was met with compassion, understanding, and acceptance.

3

Chapter 3: Stress Management Techniques

Identifying common workplace stressors

"Navigating the Rapids: Charting a Course Through Stress"

As the morning sun peeked over the horizon, casting a golden glow across the office, Sarah took a deep breath and prepared to lead her colleagues on a journey through the tumultuous waters of workplace stress.

With a furrowed brow and a determined glint in her eye, Sarah stood before her team, ready to confront the invisible adversaries that lurked in the shadows of their workplace—the common stressors that threatened to derail their journey to mental wellbeing.

She spoke of the relentless deadlines that loomed like dark clouds on the horizon, of the ever-mounting workload that threatened to overwhelm even the most seasoned professionals. She spoke of the constant pressure to perform, to meet expectations, to excel in a world that never seemed to stop moving.

As Sarah delved into the specifics of these common workplace stressors, she could feel the tension in the room rise. She saw nods of recognition and heard murmurs of agreement as her colleagues acknowledged the familiar foes that had long plagued their professional lives.

Together, they brainstormed ways to identify and address these stressors head-on, whether through time management techniques, prioritization strategies, or delegation of tasks. They discussed the importance of setting boundaries and saying no when their plates were already overflowing, recognizing that self-care was not selfish, but essential for survival.

As the meeting continued, Sarah could feel a sense of camaraderie and support begin to emerge—a shared understanding that they were all in this together, navigating the rapids of workplace stress as a united front.

As the sun climbed higher in the sky, casting a warm glow through the office windows, Sarah knew that their journey was far from over. But armed with the knowledge of how to identify and address common workplace stressors, she felt a newfound sense of confidence in their ability to weather the storm and emerge stronger on the other side.

Developing coping strategies for stress management

"Forging Resilience: Crafting Tools for the Journey Ahead"

As the midday sun illuminated the office with a warm glow, Sarah stood before her colleagues once more, ready to delve deeper into the heart of their journey—developing coping strategies to navigate the turbulent waters of workplace stress.

With a determined spark in her eyes, Sarah spoke of the importance of resilience, of the ability to weather life's storms with grace and strength. She outlined the need to develop coping strategies that would serve as lifelines in times of turmoil, anchoring them firmly amidst the chaos.

She spoke of mindfulness and meditation, of the power of grounding oneself in the present moment and finding solace in the stillness. She shared techniques for deep breathing and relaxation, guiding her colleagues through exercises designed to calm their racing minds and soothe their frayed nerves.

As Sarah delved into the specifics of these coping strategies, she could feel the tension in the room begin to dissipate, replaced by a sense of calm and clarity. She saw shoulders relax and heard sighs of relief as her colleagues embraced the tools that would help them navigate the challenges ahead.

Together, they brainstormed ways to integrate these coping strategies into their daily lives, whether through morning meditation rituals, lunchtime walks in nature, or afternoon stretching sessions to release tension from their bodies.

As the meeting continued, Sarah could feel a sense of empowerment begin to swell within her—a deep-seated belief that they were not just victims of circumstance, but masters of their own destinies. She knew that by developing coping strategies for stress management, they were forging a path to resilience, one step at a time.

As the sun began its descent toward the horizon, casting a soft, golden glow across the office, Sarah knew that their journey was far from over. But armed with the tools and techniques they had developed together, she felt a sense of hope and determination rising within her—a beacon of light to guide them through the darkness of uncertainty and into a future where they could thrive, no matter what challenges lay ahead.

Promoting work-life balance and boundaries

"Harmony Amidst Chaos: Balancing the Scales of Life"

As the evening shadows lengthened and the office grew quiet, Sarah gathered her colleagues once more, ready to explore the delicate dance of work-life balance—a dance that held the key to finding harmony amidst the chaos of modern life.

With a gentle warmth in her voice, Sarah spoke of the importance of setting boundaries, of carving out space in their lives for rest, relaxation, and rejuvenation. She emphasized the need to prioritize self-care, to nourish their minds, bodies, and spirits so that they could show up as their best selves—both at work and at home.

She shared strategies for promoting work-life balance, whether through time management techniques, boundary-setting exercises, or mindfulness practices that allowed them to savor the present moment and let go of the pressures of the past and future.

As Sarah delved into the specifics of these strategies, she could feel the tension in the room begin to ease, replaced by a sense of possibility and empowerment. She saw smiles of recognition and heard nods of agreement as her colleagues embraced the idea of reclaiming control over their time and energy.

Together, they brainstormed ways to promote work-life balance in their daily lives, whether through designated "un-plugged" evenings with family and friends, or weekends spent in nature, away from the relentless demands of technology and screens.

As the meeting continued, Sarah could feel a sense of relief wash over her—a deep-seated belief that they were not just cogs in the machine, but human beings with the power to shape their own destinies. She knew that by promoting work-life balance and boundaries, they were reclaiming their autonomy, forging a path to fulfillment and happiness on their own terms.

As the last rays of sunlight faded from the sky, casting a soft, golden glow across the office, Sarah knew that their journey was far from over. But armed with the knowledge and tools they had developed together, she felt a sense of peace and contentment settling within her—a beacon of light to guide them through the darkness of overwhelm and into a future where they could thrive, both at work and in life.

Practicing mindfulness and relaxation techniques

"Finding Calm Amidst the Storm: Embracing the Power of Mindfulness"

As the city lights twinkled outside the office windows, casting a soothing glow over the room, Sarah gathered her colleagues once more, ready to dive into the transformative world of mindfulness and relaxation techniques—a sanctuary of peace amidst the chaos of their daily lives.

With a softness in her voice and a gentle smile on her lips, Sarah spoke of the power of mindfulness, of the simple yet profound practice of being fully present in the moment. She shared stories of her own journey with mindfulness, of the moments of stillness and clarity that had anchored her amidst the storms of life.

As Sarah delved into the specifics of mindfulness and relaxation techniques, she could feel the tension in the room begin to melt away, replaced by a sense of calm and tranquility. She saw shoulders relax and heard sighs of relief as her colleagues embraced the tools that would help them find peace in the midst of chaos.

Together, they explored the practice of mindfulness meditation, guiding each other through exercises designed to anchor their attention to the present moment—to the gentle rhythm of their breath, the sensation of their feet on the ground, and the whispers of their own inner wisdom.

They also delved into the world of relaxation techniques, from progressive muscle relaxation to guided imagery, finding solace in the simple act of letting go and surrendering to the flow of life.

As the meeting continued, Sarah could feel a sense of unity and connection begin to blossom among her colleagues— a shared understanding that they were all on this journey together, navigating the ebbs and flows of life with grace and resilience.

As the city lights outside grew dimmer, casting a soft, ethereal glow over the room, Sarah knew that their journey was far from over. But armed with the tools and techniques they had cultivated together, she felt a sense of peace and contentment settle within her—a beacon of light to guide them through the darkness of uncertainty and into a future where they could thrive, anchored in the gentle embrace of mindfulness and relaxation.

Encouraging physical activity and healthy lifestyle habits

"Energizing the Spirit: Fueling the Body and Mind"

As the office hummed with the soft buzz of activity, Sarah stood before her colleagues once more, ready to embark on the next leg of their journey—encouraging physical activity and healthy lifestyle habits as pillars of strength and vitality in their quest for wellbeing.

With a vibrant energy in her voice and a sparkle in her eye, Sarah spoke of the transformative power of movement, of the simple yet profound act of nurturing their bodies through physical activity and healthy lifestyle habits.

She shared stories of her own journey with fitness, of the joy and exhilaration that came from moving her body in ways that felt nourishing and empowering. She spoke of the mental clarity and emotional resilience that she had gained through regular exercise and balanced nutrition.

As Sarah delved into the specifics of physical activity and healthy lifestyle habits, she could feel the energy in the room begin to shift, replaced by a sense of excitement and determination. She saw smiles of anticipation and heard murmurs of agreement as her colleagues embraced the idea of prioritizing their health and wellbeing.

Together, they brainstormed ways to incorporate physical activity into their daily lives, whether through lunchtime walks, after-work yoga sessions, or weekend hikes in nature. They discussed the importance of nourishing their bodies with wholesome, nutrient-rich foods, fueling themselves for optimal performance and vitality.

As the meeting continued, Sarah could feel a sense of empowerment begin to swell within her—a deep-seated belief that they were not just passive observers of their health, but active participants in their own wellbeing. She knew that by encouraging physical activity and healthy lifestyle habits, they were laying the foundation for a future filled with vitality and strength.

As the sun dipped below the horizon, casting a warm, golden glow over the room, Sarah knew that their journey was far from over. But armed with the knowledge and enthusiasm they had cultivated together, she felt a sense of excitement and anticipation rising within her—a beacon of light to guide them on their path to health and happiness, one step at a time.

Seeking professional support for stress-related issues

"Embracing Support: Reaching Out in Times of Need"

As the day drew to a close and the office settled into a hushed calm, Sarah gathered her colleagues once more, ready to explore the vital importance of seeking professional support for stress-related issues—a beacon of hope in the darkest of nights.

With a gentle compassion in her voice and a softness in her gaze, Sarah spoke of the courage it took to reach out for help, to acknowledge that sometimes, the burdens of life were too heavy to bear alone. She shared stories of her own journey with professional support, of the healing and transformation that had come from seeking guidance and assistance when she needed it most.

As Sarah delved into the specifics of seeking professional support for stress-related issues, she could feel the vulnerability in the room begin to surface, replaced by a sense of acceptance and understanding. She saw nods of recognition and heard whispers of solidarity as her colleagues embraced the idea of reaching out for help when they needed it most.

Together, they explored the various avenues for seeking professional support, whether through therapy, counseling, or psychiatric services. They discussed the importance of finding a therapist or counselor who resonated with their needs and values, creating a safe space for healing and growth.

As the meeting continued, Sarah could feel a sense of relief wash over her—a deep-seated belief that they were not alone in their struggles, but surrounded by a network of support and compassion. She knew that by seeking professional support for stress-related issues, they were taking a courageous step toward healing and wholeness.

As the office lights dimmed and the city outside settled into a gentle slumber, Sarah knew that their journey was far from over. But armed with the knowledge and courage they had cultivated together, she felt a sense of peace and reassurance settling within her—a beacon of light to guide them through the darkness of uncertainty and into a future where they could thrive, supported by the unwavering strength of professional care and compassion.

4

Chapter 4: Building Resilience

Understanding resilience and its importance in the workplace

"Rising Strong: Building Resilience in the Workplace"

As the dawn painted the sky with hues of pink and gold, Sarah gathered her colleagues once more, ready to embark on a journey through the transformative landscape of resilience—a beacon of strength in the face of adversity.

With a sense of reverence in her voice and a glimmer of determination in her eyes, Sarah spoke of resilience—the steadfast resilience that allowed individuals to bounce back from setbacks, to rise stronger and wiser in the face of adversity.

She shared stories of triumph and triumph over adversity, of individuals who had weathered the storms of life with grace and resilience, emerging victorious on the other side. She spoke of the importance of resilience in the workplace, of its role in fostering innovation, collaboration, and growth.

As Sarah delved into the specifics of resilience and its importance in the workplace, she could feel the energy in the room shift, replaced by a sense of curiosity and intrigue. She saw heads nodding in agreement and heard murmurs of recognition as her colleagues embraced the idea of resilience as a cornerstone of success in their professional lives.

Together, they explored the various components of resilience, from adaptability and flexibility to perseverance and optimism. They discussed the importance of cultivating a growth mindset, of viewing challenges as opportunities for learning and growth rather than obstacles to be overcome.

As the meeting continued, Sarah could feel a sense of empowerment begin to swell within her—a deep-seated belief that they were not just passive victims of circumstance, but active architects of their own destinies. She knew that by understanding resilience and its importance in the workplace, they were laying the foundation for a future filled with possibility and promise.

As the sun climbed higher in the sky, casting a warm, golden glow over the room, Sarah knew that their journey was far from over. But armed with the knowledge and determination they had cultivated together, she felt a sense of excitement and anticipation rising within her—a beacon of light to guide them through the challenges that lay ahead, with resilience as their guiding star.

Cultivating Self-awareness and emotional intelligence

"The Heart of Strength: Nurturing Self-Awareness and Emotional Intelligence"

As the morning light streamed through the windows, illuminating the room with a gentle glow, Sarah stood before her colleagues once more, ready to delve into the transformative power of self-awareness and emotional intelligence—a beacon of insight and understanding in the ever-changing landscape of the workplace.

With a tender warmth in her voice and a softness in her gaze, Sarah spoke of the importance of knowing oneself, of cultivating a deep sense of self-awareness that allowed individuals to navigate the complexities of their emotions with grace and wisdom.

She shared stories of individuals who had embraced their emotions with open arms, who had leaned into discomfort and uncertainty, emerging stronger and more resilient on the other side. She spoke of the power of emotional intelligence— the ability to recognize, understand, and manage one's own emotions, as well as those of others.

As Sarah delved into the specifics of self-awareness and emotional intelligence, she could feel the energy in the room begin to shift, replaced by a sense of introspection and curiosity. She saw furrowed brows soften and heard murmurs of recognition as her colleagues embraced the idea of diving deep into the ocean of their own emotions.

Together, they explored techniques for cultivating self-awareness, from mindfulness practices to journaling exercises that allowed them to reflect on their thoughts and feelings. They discussed the importance of empathy and compassion in building emotional intelligence, of tuning into the emotions of others and responding with kindness and understanding.

As the meeting continued, Sarah could feel a sense of connection begin to blossom among her colleagues—a shared understanding that they were all on this journey together, navigating the peaks and valleys of their emotions with courage and resilience.

As the sun climbed higher in the sky, casting a warm, golden glow over the room, Sarah knew that their journey was far from over. But armed with the tools and insights they had cultivated together, she felt a sense of peace and reassurance settling within her—a beacon of light to guide them through the twists and turns of their emotional landscapes, with self-awareness and emotional intelligence as their guiding stars.

Developing problem-solving and adaptability skills

"Navigating the Unknown: Harnessing the Power of Adaptability and Problem-Solving"

As the day progressed and the office bustled with activity, Sarah reconvened her colleagues once more, ready to explore the dynamic realms of problem-solving and adaptability—a beacon of resilience in the face of uncertainty.

With a determined fervor in her voice and a sparkle of anticipation in her eyes, Sarah spoke of the importance of flexibility and innovation in the ever-evolving landscape of the workplace. She shared stories of individuals who had embraced change with open arms, who had thrived in the face of uncertainty by tapping into their problem-solving skills and adaptability.

She spoke of the need to cultivate a growth mindset, of viewing challenges as opportunities for learning and growth rather than obstacles to be overcome. She emphasized the importance of developing problem-solving skills, of approaching problems with creativity and resourcefulness to find innovative solutions.

As Sarah delved into the specifics of problem-solving and adaptability, she could feel the energy in the room shift, replaced by a sense of excitement and possibility. She saw heads nodding in agreement and heard murmurs of determination as her colleagues embraced the idea of embracing change as a catalyst for growth.

Together, they explored techniques for developing problem-solving skills, from brainstorming sessions to design thinking exercises that encouraged them to think outside the box. They discussed the importance of embracing uncertainty and ambiguity, of adapting quickly to changing circumstances with resilience and grace.

As the meeting continued, Sarah could feel a sense of empowerment begin to swell within her—a deep-seated belief that they were not just passive observers of their circumstances, but active agents of change. She knew that by developing problem-solving and adaptability skills, they were laying the foundation for a future filled with resilience and success.

As the sun began to set, casting a warm, golden glow over the room, Sarah knew that their journey was far from over. But armed with the knowledge and determination they had cultivated together, she felt a sense of optimism and excitement rising within her—a beacon of light to guide them through the twists and turns of their professional lives, with problem-solving and adaptability as their guiding stars.

Fostering positive relationships and social support networks

"Strength in Unity: Nurturing Bonds and Building Bridges"

As the evening descended and the office began to quieten, Sarah called her colleagues together once more, ready to explore the transformative power of positive relationships and social support networks—a beacon of solidarity in the midst of life's storms.

With a gentle warmth in her voice and a softness in her gaze, Sarah spoke of the importance of connection, of building bonds that served as anchors in times of need. She shared stories of individuals who had found strength in the embrace of their social support networks, who had weathered life's challenges with the unwavering support of their friends, family, and colleagues.

She spoke of the need to cultivate positive relationships in the workplace, of fostering an environment where kindness and compassion flourished, and where every individual felt seen, heard, and valued. She emphasized the importance of reaching out for support when needed, of leaning on others for strength and guidance in times of struggle.

As Sarah delved into the specifics of fostering positive relationships and social support networks, she could feel the energy in the room shift, replaced by a sense of camaraderie and connection. She saw smiles of recognition and heard nods of agreement as her colleagues embraced the idea of building bridges that spanned the divides of distance and difference.

Together, they brainstormed ways to nurture positive relationships in the workplace, whether through team-building activities, mentorship programs, or simply taking the time to check in with one another on a regular basis. They discussed the importance of creating a culture of support and collaboration, where every individual felt empowered to reach out for help without fear of judgment or stigma.

As the meeting continued, Sarah could feel a sense of unity begin to blossom among her colleagues—a shared understanding that they were all in this together, navigating the highs and lows of life as a united front.

As the office lights dimmed and the city outside settled into a gentle slumber, Sarah knew that their journey was far from over. But armed with the bonds of connection they had forged together, she felt a sense of peace and reassurance settling within her—a beacon of light to guide them through the darkness of uncertainty and into a future where they could thrive, supported by the strength of their social support networks.

Learning from setbacks and failures

"Rising Strong: Embracing the Lessons of Setbacks"

As the day waned and the office grew quiet, Sarah called her colleagues together once more, ready to explore the transformative power of learning from setbacks and failures—a beacon of resilience in the face of adversity.

With a determined resolve in her voice and a glimmer of resilience in her eyes, Sarah spoke of the inevitability of setbacks and failures in the journey toward success. She shared stories of individuals who had stumbled and fallen, only to rise stronger and wiser from the ashes of defeat.

She spoke of the importance of reframing setbacks as opportunities for growth, of embracing failure as a teacher rather than a punishment. She emphasized the need to cultivate resilience in the face of adversity, to dust oneself off and forge ahead with courage and determination.

As Sarah delved into the specifics of learning from setbacks and failures, she could feel the tension in the room ease, replaced by a sense of acceptance and understanding. She saw nods of recognition and heard whispers of solidarity as her colleagues embraced the idea of embracing failure as a stepping stone to success.

Together, they explored techniques for learning from setbacks, from reflection exercises to seeking feedback from peers and mentors. They discussed the importance of resilience in bouncing back from failure, of refusing to let setbacks define their worth or determine their destiny.

As the meeting continued, Sarah could feel a sense of empowerment begin to swell within her—a deep-seated belief that they were not just victims of circumstance, but architects of their own destinies. She knew that by learning from setbacks and failures, they were laying the foundation for a future filled with resilience and triumph.

As the last rays of sunlight faded from the sky, casting a soft, ethereal glow over the room, Sarah knew that their journey was far from over. But armed with the knowledge and determination they had cultivated together, she felt a sense of hope and possibility rising within her—a beacon of light to guide them through the darkest of nights, with resilience as their guiding star.

Promoting a growth mindset and optimism

"The Power of Possibility: Cultivating Growth and Optimism"

As the night settled in, bathing the office in a gentle glow, Sarah gathered her colleagues once more, ready to explore the transformative landscape of promoting a growth mindset and optimism—a beacon of hope in the face of uncertainty.

With a radiant warmth in her voice and a sparkle of optimism in her eyes, Sarah spoke of the power of possibility, of the boundless potential that lay within each and every one of them. She shared stories of individuals who had embraced a growth mindset, who had refused to be limited by their circumstances and had instead chosen to see challenges as opportunities for growth.

She spoke of the importance of cultivating optimism in the face of adversity, of viewing setbacks as temporary roadblocks rather than insurmountable obstacles. She emphasized the need to foster a sense of hope and possibility in the workplace, to create an environment where every individual felt empowered to dream big and reach for the stars.

As Sarah delved into the specifics of promoting a growth mindset and optimism, she could feel the energy in the room shift, replaced by a sense of excitement and determination. She saw smiles of anticipation and heard murmurs of agreement as her colleagues embraced the idea of embracing possibility with open arms.

Together, they explored techniques for cultivating a growth mindset, from reframing negative thoughts to seeking out new challenges that stretched their abilities. They discussed the importance of fostering optimism in the face of adversity, of finding silver linings in even the darkest of clouds.

As the meeting continued, Sarah could feel a sense of possibility begin to blossom among her colleagues—a shared understanding that they were not just passive bystanders in their own lives, but active participants in the creation of their own destinies.

As the night deepened and the stars twinkled in the sky outside, Sarah knew that their journey was far from over. But armed with the belief in the power of growth and optimism, she felt a sense of excitement and anticipation rising within her—a beacon of light to guide them through the challenges that lay ahead, with boundless possibility as their guiding star.

5

Chapter 5: Addressing Burnout

Recognizing signs and symptoms of burnout

"Fanning the Flames: Confronting Burnout with Courage"

As the office buzzed with the energy of a new day, Sarah called her colleagues together once more, ready to tackle the formidable challenge of addressing burnout—a beacon of resilience in the face of exhaustion.

With a compassionate tone in her voice and a gentle concern in her eyes, Sarah spoke of the insidious nature of burnout, of the toll it could take on their mental, emotional, and physical wellbeing. She shared stories of individuals who had fallen victim to burnout, who had pushed themselves to the brink of exhaustion in pursuit of success, only to find themselves depleted and disillusioned.

She spoke of the importance of recognizing the signs and symptoms of burnout, of tuning into the whispers of their own bodies and minds before they escalated into shouts of distress.

She emphasized the need to pay attention to warning signs such as chronic fatigue, decreased motivation, and feelings of cynicism or detachment.

As Sarah delved into the specifics of recognizing signs and symptoms of burnout, she could feel the tension in the room rise, replaced by a sense of unease and vulnerability. She saw furrowed brows and heard murmurs of recognition as her colleagues grappled with the realization that they too could be susceptible to burnout.

Together, they explored techniques for recognizing and addressing burnout, from regular self-assessments to open and honest conversations with trusted colleagues or mentors. They discussed the importance of setting boundaries and prioritizing self-care, of recognizing that their worth was not defined by their productivity or achievements.

As the meeting continued, Sarah could feel a sense of solidarity begin to blossom among her colleagues—a shared understanding that they were all in this together, navigating the turbulent waters of burnout with courage and resilience.

As the sun climbed higher in the sky, casting a warm, golden glow over the room, Sarah knew that their journey was far from over. But armed with the knowledge and awareness they had cultivated together, she felt a sense of hope rising within her—a beacon of light to guide them through the darkness of burnout and into a future where they could thrive, with compassion and self-care as their guiding lights.

Understanding the causes of burnout in the workplace

"Unraveling the Threads: Exploring the Roots of Workplace Burnout"

As the day progressed and the office hummed with activity, Sarah reconvened her colleagues once more, ready to unravel the complex tapestry of workplace burnout—a beacon of understanding in the midst of confusion.

With a determined resolve in her voice and a keen curiosity in her eyes, Sarah spoke of the myriad factors that could contribute to burnout in the workplace. She shared stories of individuals who had found themselves overwhelmed and exhausted by the relentless demands of their jobs, struggling to find balance amidst the chaos.

She spoke of the importance of understanding the root causes of burnout, of peeling back the layers to reveal the underlying factors that could undermine their wellbeing. She emphasized the need to address issues such as excessive workload, lack of autonomy, and poor work-life balance, which could all contribute to burnout.

As Sarah delved into the specifics of understanding the causes of burnout in the workplace, she could feel the tension in the room rise, replaced by a sense of recognition and empathy. She saw nods of understanding and heard murmurs of agreement as her colleagues grappled with the realization that they too had experienced the strain of burnout.

Together, they explored the various factors that could contribute to burnout, from toxic workplace cultures to ineffective leadership practices. They discussed the importance of creating environments where individuals felt supported and valued, where their contributions were recognized and their wellbeing was prioritized.

As the meeting continued, Sarah could feel a sense of solidarity begin to emerge among her colleagues—a shared commitment to uncovering the root causes of burnout and creating workplaces where everyone could thrive.

As the sun dipped below the horizon, casting a warm, golden glow over the room, Sarah knew that their journey was far from over. But armed with the knowledge and insight they had cultivated together, she felt a sense of optimism rising within her—a beacon of light to guide them through the shadows of burnout and into a future where they could flourish, with understanding and empathy as their guiding stars.

Creating a culture of work-life balance and self-care

"Harmony Amidst the Hustle: Cultivating a Culture of Balance and Care"

As the day drew on and the office buzzed with activity, Sarah once again called her colleagues together, ready to explore the vital importance of creating a culture of work-life balance and self-care—a beacon of harmony in the midst of chaos.

With a gentle determination in her voice and a softness in her gaze, Sarah spoke of the need to foster an environment where work and life could exist in harmony, where individuals felt empowered to prioritize their wellbeing without fear of judgment or retribution. She shared stories of organizations that had embraced a culture of balance bund care, where flexible schedules, remote work options, and wellness programs were the norm rather than the exception.

She spoke of the importance of setting boundaries and creating rituals that nurtured their physical, emotional, and mental health. She emphasized the need to destigmatize self-care and prioritize rest and rejuvenation as essential components of productivity and success.

As Sarah delved into the specifics of creating a culture of work-life balance and self-care, she could feel the energy in the room shift, replaced by a sense of possibility and hope. She saw heads nodding in agreement and heard murmurs of approval as her colleagues embraced the idea of prioritizing their wellbeing in the workplace.

Together, they brainstormed ways to foster a culture of balance and care, from implementing flexible work hours to offering wellness workshops and mindfulness sessions. They discussed the importance of leading by example, of modeling healthy behaviors and encouraging open conversations about self-care.

As the meeting continued, Sarah could feel a sense of empowerment begin to swell within her—a deep-seated belief that they had the power to create a workplace where everyone could thrive, supported by a culture of balance and care.

As the sun began to set, casting a warm, golden glow over the room, Sarah knew that their journey was far from over. But armed with the vision and determination they had cultivated together, she felt a sense of optimism rising within her—a beacon of light to guide them through the challenges of burnout and into a future where they could flourish, with balance and care as their guiding principles.

Setting realistic goals and expectations

"Navigating the Unknown: Balancing Ambition with Realism"

As the shadows lengthened and the office quieted, Sarah gathered her colleagues once more, prepared to navigate the delicate balance of setting realistic goals and expectations—a beacon of wisdom in the realm of ambition and uncertainty.

With a thoughtful tone in her voice and a glimmer of determination in her eyes, Sarah spoke of the importance of setting goals that were both ambitious and achievable. She shared stories of individuals who had pushed themselves to the brink in pursuit of their dreams, only to find themselves overwhelmed and burnt out by unrealistic expectations.

She spoke of the need to balance ambition with realism, to set goals that stretched their abilities without sacrificing their wellbeing. She emphasized the importance of taking calculated risks, of stepping into the unknown with faith as their guide, but also acknowledging the importance of setting boundaries and prioritizing self-care along the way.

As Sarah delved into the specifics of setting realistic goals and expectations, she could feel the tension in the room rise, replaced by a sense of introspection and contemplation. She saw furrowed brows and heard murmurs of recognition as her colleagues grappled with the realization that they too had fallen prey to the allure of unrealistic expectations.

Together, they explored techniques for setting realistic goals, from breaking larger objectives into smaller, more manageable tasks to seeking feedback from peers and mentors. They discussed the importance of balancing ambition with self-awareness, of knowing their own limitations and respecting their boundaries.

As the meeting continued, Sarah could feel a sense of clarity begin to emerge among her colleagues—a shared understanding that while ambition was essential for growth and success, it must be tempered with realism and self-care.

As the moon rose high in the sky, casting a soft, ethereal glow over the room, Sarah knew that their journey was far from over. But armed with the wisdom and insight they had cultivated together, she felt a sense of peace settling within her—a beacon of light to guide them through the uncertainties of the unknown, with balance and faith as their guiding stars.

Encouraging breaks and time off

"The Pause that Refreshes: Embracing Rest and Renewal"

As the day faded into evening and the office gradually quieted, Sarah called her colleagues together once more, ready to explore the importance of encouraging breaks and time off—a beacon of rejuvenation in the midst of relentless workdays.

With a gentle insistence in her voice and a warmth in her demeanor, Sarah spoke of the necessity of embracing rest and renewal in the pursuit of long-term success and wellbeing. She shared stories of individuals who had neglected their own needs, sacrificing their health and happiness on the altar of productivity.

She spoke of the importance of taking breaks and time off, of allowing themselves the space to recharge and replenish their energy reserves. She emphasized that breaks were not signs of weakness, but essential components of a healthy and sustainable work-life balance.

As Sarah delved into the specifics of encouraging breaks and time off, she could feel the tension in the room ease, replaced by a sense of relief and permission. She saw shoulders relax and heard sighs of agreement as her colleagues embraced the idea of prioritizing their own wellbeing.

Together, they brainstormed ways to encourage breaks and time off in the workplace, from implementing policies that mandated regular breaks to fostering a culture where taking time off was not only accepted but encouraged. They discussed the importance of leading by example, of modeling healthy behaviors and demonstrating that breaks were not only acceptable but necessary for peak performance.

As the meeting continued, Sarah could feel a sense of liberation begin to emerge among her colleagues—a shared understanding that they were not slaves to their work, but sovereign beings with the right to rest and rejuvenate as needed.

As the stars began to twinkle in the night sky, casting a soft, comforting glow over the room, Sarah knew that their journey was far from over. But armed with the knowledge and permission they had cultivated together, she felt a sense of peace settling within her—a beacon of light to guide them through the challenges of burnout and into a future where they could thrive, with rest and renewal as their guiding principles.

Providing resources for managing and preventing burnout

"Arming Against the Storm: Equipping with Resources for Burnout Prevention"

As the office settled into a quiet rhythm, Sarah convened her colleagues once more, prepared to equip them with the tools and resources needed to manage and prevent burnout—a beacon of resilience in the face of adversity.

With a sense of urgency in her voice and a determination in her eyes, Sarah spoke of the importance of arming themselves against the storm of burnout with a wealth of resources and support systems. She shared stories of individuals who had found solace and strength in the guidance and assistance of counselors, therapists, and wellness programs.

She spoke of the need to create a comprehensive support network that addressed the multifaceted nature of burnout, from mental health resources to stress management techniques. She emphasized that no one should have to face burnout alone and that help was always available for those who sought it.

As Sarah delved into the specifics of providing resources for managing and preventing burnout, she could feel the tension in the room ease, replaced by a sense of reassurance and empowerment. She saw nods of understanding and heard murmurs of appreciation as her colleagues embraced the idea of reaching out for support when needed.

Together, they brainstormed ways to provide resources for managing and preventing burnout in the workplace, from offering employee assistance programs to organizing wellness workshops and seminars. They discussed the importance of creating a culture where seeking help was not only accepted but encouraged, where every individual felt supported and valued.

As the meeting continued, Sarah could feel a sense of solidarity begin to emerge among her colleagues—a shared commitment to arming themselves against burnout and creating workplaces where everyone could thrive.

As the night deepened and the stars twinkled in the sky outside, casting a soft, comforting glow over the room, Sarah knew that their journey was far from over. But armed with the resources and support they had cultivated together, she felt a sense of confidence rising within her—a beacon of light to guide them through the storms of burnout and into a future where they could flourish, supported by the unwavering strength of their collective resilience.

6

Chapter 6: Promoting Psychological Safety

Defining psychological safety and its impact on workplace mental health

"Building Trust, Fostering Growth: Nurturing Psychological Safety in the Workplace"

As the morning sun cast its warm glow upon the office, Sarah gathered her colleagues once more, poised to delve into the crucial topic of promoting psychological safety—a beacon of trust and support in the fabric of the workplace.

With a gentle yet resolute tone in her voice and a gleam of conviction in her eyes, Sarah began to unravel the concept of psychological safety and its profound influence on the mental health of individuals in the workplace. She shared stories of teams that had flourished in environments where trust and openness thrived, where every voice was valued and respected.

She spoke of psychological safety as the bedrock upon which healthy workplace relationships were built—a space where individuals felt secure enough to take risks, express their thoughts and ideas without fear of judgment, and admit mistakes without repercussions. She emphasized its role in fostering innovation, collaboration, and employee well-being.

As Sarah delved into the specifics of defining psychological safety and its impact on workplace mental health, she could sense the room coming alive with recognition and understanding. She observed nods of agreement and heard murmurs of affirmation as her colleagues began to grasp the profound implications of this foundational concept.

Together, they explored the ripple effects of psychological safety on individual and organizational well-being, from reduced stress and anxiety to increased engagement and productivity. They discussed the transformative power of creating an environment where authenticity and vulnerability were not only accepted but celebrated.

As the meeting continued, Sarah could feel a sense of solidarity and purpose blossoming among her colleagues—a shared commitment to fostering psychological safety and building a workplace culture where everyone could thrive.

As the sun reached its zenith in the sky, casting a warm, golden glow over the room, Sarah knew that their journey was just beginning. But armed with the understanding and determination they had cultivated together, she felt a sense of optimism rising within her—a beacon of light to guide them as they embarked on the path toward a more supportive and inclusive workplace, where psychological safety reigned supreme.

Building trust and open communication among team members

"Bridging Bonds, Building Trust: Fostering Open Communication in Teams"

As the day unfolded and the office buzzed with activity, Sarah reconvened her colleagues once more, ready to explore the essential task of building trust and fostering open communication—a beacon of connection in the heart of the workplace.

With a warm yet determined demeanor, Sarah embarked on unraveling the intricate dance of trust and communication within teams. She shared stories of groups that had thrived on foundations of mutual respect and open dialogue, where every member felt heard, valued, and supported.

She spoke of trust as the cornerstone of effective teamwork—a delicate bond that was nurtured through transparency, reliability, and empathy. She emphasized the importance of cultivating an environment where team members felt safe to express their thoughts, opinions, and concerns without fear of judgment or reprisal.

As Sarah delved into the specifics of building trust and open communication among team members, she could feel the energy in the room shift, replaced by a sense of camaraderie and understanding. She saw nods of agreement and heard murmurs of recognition as her colleagues recognized the vital role that trust played in their collaborative efforts.

Together, they explored techniques for fostering trust and open communication, from regular team-building exercises to establishing clear channels for feedback and discussion. They discussed the importance of active listening, empathy, and vulnerability in building strong interpersonal connections within teams.

As the meeting continued, Sarah could feel a sense of unity begin to blossom among her colleagues—a shared commitment to building trust and fostering open communication as pillars of their collective success.

As the sun dipped below the horizon, casting a warm, golden glow over the room, Sarah knew that their journey was far from over. But armed with the bonds of trust and communication they had cultivated together, she felt a sense of confidence rising within her—a beacon of light to guide them through the challenges of collaboration and into a future where they could achieve greatness, united in purpose and solidarity.

Encouraging constructive feedback and vulnerability

"Embracing Growth, Nurturing Vulnerability: Fostering Constructive Feedback"

As the office settled into a steady rhythm, Sarah called her colleagues together once more, ready to explore the transformative power of encouraging constructive feedback and vulnerability—a beacon of growth in the heart of collaboration.

With a blend of warmth and determination in her voice, Sarah embarked on unraveling the delicate dance of feedback and vulnerability within teams. She shared stories of groups that had flourished on foundations of openness and honesty, where constructive criticism was embraced as an opportunity for growth rather than a threat.

She spoke of vulnerability as the bridge that connected individuals, allowing them to forge deeper connections and foster trust within their teams. She emphasized the importance of creating an environment where team members felt safe to share their ideas, thoughts, and concerns openly, knowing that they would be met with empathy and support.

As Sarah delved into the specifics of encouraging constructive feedback and vulnerability, she could feel the energy in the room shift, replaced by a sense of anticipation and curiosity. She saw heads nodding in agreement and heard murmurs of recognition as her colleagues embraced the idea of embracing vulnerability as a catalyst for growth.

Together, they explored techniques for fostering constructive feedback and vulnerability, from establishing regular feedback sessions to creating a culture where mistakes were viewed as opportunities for learning rather than sources of shame. They discussed the importance of humility and openness in giving and receiving feedback, and the transformative power of vulnerability in building stronger, more resilient teams.

As the meeting continued, Sarah could feel a sense of connection begin to blossom among her colleagues—a shared commitment to embracing vulnerability and fostering a culture of constructive feedback as pillars of their collective success.

As the sun began to set, casting a warm, golden glow over the room, Sarah knew that their journey was far from over. But armed with the courage and vulnerability they had cultivated together, she felt a sense of optimism rising within her— a beacon of light to guide them through the challenges of collaboration and into a future where they could achieve greatness, united in authenticity and trust.

Addressing bullying, harassment, and discrimination

"Standing Tall, Erasing Shadows: Confronting Bullying, Harassment, and Discrimination"

As the day progressed and the office hummed with activity, Sarah reconvened her colleagues once more, prepared to confront the shadows of bullying, harassment, and discrimination—a beacon of courage in the face of adversity.

With a steely resolve in her voice and a fire of determination in her eyes, Sarah embarked on unraveling the dark threads of bullying, harassment, and discrimination that threatened the fabric of their workplace. She shared stories of individuals who had suffered in silence, their voices stifled by fear and shame, their spirits crushed by the weight of injustice.

She spoke of the imperative to create a workplace where every individual felt safe, respected, and valued—a space where bullying, harassment, and discrimination had no place to hide. She emphasized the importance of standing up against injustice, of speaking out against behavior that demeaned and dehumanized others.

As Sarah delved into the specifics of addressing bullying, harassment, and discrimination, she could feel the tension in the room rise, replaced by a sense of urgency and determination. She saw jaws set in determination and heard murmurs of agreement as her colleagues embraced the idea of eradicating toxicity from their workplace.

Together, they explored techniques for addressing bullying, harassment, and discrimination, from implementing clear policies and procedures to providing training and education on diversity and inclusion. They discussed the importance of creating a culture where every individual felt empowered to speak up against injustice, knowing that their voices would be heard and respected.

As the meeting continued, Sarah could feel a sense of solidarity and defiance begin to emerge among her colleagues—a shared commitment to standing tall against bullying, harassment, and discrimination, and creating a workplace where everyone could thrive.

As the sun dipped below the horizon, casting a warm, golden glow over the room, Sarah knew that their journey was far from over. But armed with the courage and determination they had cultivated together, she felt a sense of hope rising within her—a beacon of light to guide them through the darkness of injustice and into a future where equality and respect reigned supreme.

Empowering employees to speak up about mental health concerns

"Voices of Courage, Seeds of Change: Empowering Mental Health Advocacy"

As the office settled into a hushed anticipation, Sarah called her colleagues together once more, ready to empower them to speak up about mental health concerns—a beacon of courage in the realm of advocacy and support.

With a gentle determination in her voice and a glimmer of empathy in her eyes, Sarah embarked on unraveling the stigma surrounding mental health in the workplace. She shared stories of individuals who had struggled in silence, their voices stifled by shame and fear of judgment, their mental health concerns left unaddressed and unresolved.

She spoke of the imperative to create a culture where every individual felt empowered to speak openly about their mental health, knowing that they would be met with compassion and support. She emphasized the importance of breaking down barriers to communication, of fostering an environment where vulnerability was seen as a strength rather than a weakness.

As Sarah delved into the specifics of empowering employees to speak up about mental health concerns, she could feel the room brimming with anticipation, replaced by a sense of possibility and liberation. She saw nods of understanding and heard murmurs of agreement as her colleagues embraced the idea of advocating for their mental health rights.

Together, they explored techniques for empowering mental health advocacy, from providing education and resources to creating safe spaces for open dialogue and support. They discussed the importance of leading by example, of sharing their own stories and experiences to inspire others to speak up and seek help when needed.

As the meeting continued, Sarah could feel a sense of empowerment and solidarity begin to emerge among her colleagues—a shared commitment to breaking the silence surrounding mental health and creating a workplace where everyone felt seen, heard, and supported.

As the sun dipped below the horizon, casting a warm, golden glow over the room, Sarah knew that their journey was far from over. But armed with the voices of courage they had cultivated together, she felt a sense of hope rising within her—a beacon of light to guide them through the shadows of stigma and into a future where mental health was embraced and celebrated as an integral part of their collective well-being.

Creating a culture of respect, empathy, and support

"Harmony in Humanity: Cultivating Respect, Empathy, and Support"

As the day waned and the office embraced a tranquil ambiance, Sarah called her colleagues together once more, poised to foster a culture of respect, empathy, and support—a beacon of humanity in the fabric of their workplace.

With a gentle yet unwavering resolve in her voice and a glow of compassion in her eyes, Sarah embarked on unraveling the essence of respect, empathy, and support within their workplace. She shared stories of teams that had thrived amidst diversity and inclusivity, where every individual felt valued and understood.

She spoke of respect as the cornerstone of a healthy workplace culture—a fundamental principle that underpinned all interactions and relationships. She emphasized the importance of empathy in fostering understanding and connection, of walking in each other's shoes and seeing the world through their eyes.

As Sarah delved into the specifics of creating a culture of respect, empathy, and support, she could feel the room suffused with warmth and understanding, replaced by a sense of unity and solidarity. She saw smiles of recognition and heard murmurs of agreement as her colleagues embraced the idea of building a community founded on mutual respect and care.

Together, they brainstormed ways to infuse their workplace with respect, empathy, and support, from promoting diversity and inclusion initiatives to implementing peer support programs and mentorship opportunities. They discussed the importance of fostering a sense of belonging, where every individual felt valued and supported in their journey.

As the meeting continued, Sarah could feel a sense of harmony and camaraderie begin to emerge among her colleagues—a shared commitment to nurturing a culture of respect, empathy, and support as the bedrock of their collective well-being.

As the sun dipped below the horizon, casting a soft, ethereal glow over the room, Sarah knew that their journey was far from over. But armed with the principles of respect, empathy, and support they had cultivated together, she felt a sense of optimism rising within her—a beacon of light to guide them through the challenges of collaboration and into a future where humanity reigned supreme.

7

Chapter 7: Supporting Employees with Mental Health Conditions

Understanding different mental health conditions

"Embracing Diversity, Nurturing Well-being: Understanding Mental Health Conditions"

As the office hummed with a quiet anticipation, Sarah gathered her colleagues once more, ready to explore the intricacies of supporting employees with mental health conditions—a beacon of understanding in the realm of diversity and well-being.

With a gentle yet earnest tone in her voice and a glint of curiosity in her eyes, Sarah embarked on unraveling the multifaceted landscape of mental health conditions within their workplace. She shared stories of individuals who had grappled with depression, anxiety, and other mental health challenges, their journeys marked by both resilience and vulnerability.

She spoke of the imperative to cultivate empathy and understanding for those navigating mental health conditions—a commitment to seeing beyond the surface and embracing the complexity of human experiences. She emphasized the importance of education and awareness in breaking down stigmas and fostering a culture of acceptance and support.

As Sarah delved into the specifics of understanding different mental health conditions, she could feel the room come alive with curiosity and compassion, replaced by a sense of openness and receptivity. She saw nods of recognition and heard murmurs of agreement as her colleagues embraced the idea of learning and growing together.

Together, they explored the nuances of various mental health conditions, from mood disorders to psychotic disorders, from anxiety disorders to trauma-related disorders. They discussed the impact of these conditions on individuals' daily lives and their potential manifestations in the workplace.

As the meeting continued, Sarah could feel a sense of empathy and solidarity begin to blossom among her colleagues—a shared commitment to supporting each other through the highs and lows of mental health challenges.

As the sun dipped below the horizon, casting a warm, golden glow over the room, Sarah knew that their journey was far from over. But armed with the understanding and compassion they had cultivated together, she felt a sense of hope rising within her—a beacon of light to guide them through the complexities of mental health and into a future where everyone felt seen, heard, and supported.

Providing accomodations and support for employees with mental illnesses

"Empowering Every Journey: Providing Accommodations for Mental Wellness"

As the office settled into a serene atmosphere, Sarah convened her colleagues once more, prepared to delve deeper into the realm of supporting employees with mental illnesses—a beacon of empowerment in the realm of accommodation and care.

With a compassionate yet determined tone in her voice and a spark of advocacy in her eyes, Sarah embarked on unraveling the vital role of accommodations and support for employees navigating mental illnesses. She shared stories of individuals who had faced barriers and challenges in the workplace, their struggles exacerbated by a lack of understanding and accommodation.

She spoke of the imperative to create a workplace where every individual felt supported and empowered to thrive, regardless of their mental health status. She emphasized the importance of providing accommodations that met the unique needs of each individual, fostering an environment where everyone could contribute their best work.

As Sarah delved into the specifics of providing accommodations and support for employees with mental illnesses, she could feel the room brimming with empathy and determination, replaced by a sense of solidarity and commitment. She saw heads nodding in agreement and heard murmurs of affirmation as her colleagues embraced the idea of advocating for inclusivity and accessibility.

Together, they brainstormed ways to provide accommodations and support for employees with mental illnesses, from flexible work arrangements to access to mental health resources and support networks. They discussed the importance of fostering a culture of openness and understanding, where individuals felt comfortable disclosing their mental health status and seeking the help they needed.

As the meeting continued, Sarah could feel a sense of empowerment and compassion begin to blossom among her colleagues—a shared commitment to creating a workplace where everyone felt valued and supported on their journey to wellness.

As the sun dipped below the horizon, casting a soft, comforting glow over the room, Sarah knew that their journey was far from over. But armed with the advocacy and support they had cultivated together, she felt a sense of optimism rising within her—a beacon of light to guide them through the challenges of accommodation and into a future where everyone could thrive, supported by the unwavering strength of their collective compassion.

Educating managers and colleagues on mental health awareness and sensitivity

"Enlightening Minds, Fostering Understanding: Educating for Mental Health Sensitivity"

As the day unfolded and the office embraced a serene ambiance, Sarah once again gathered her colleagues, poised to explore the transformative power of educating managers and colleagues on mental health awareness—a beacon of enlightenment in the realm of sensitivity and support.

With a gentle yet resolute tone in her voice and a glimmer of enlightenment in her eyes, Sarah embarked on unraveling the importance of education in fostering a workplace culture of understanding and support for mental health. She shared stories of individuals who had faced judgment and misunderstanding, their struggles exacerbated by a lack of awareness and sensitivity.

She spoke of the imperative to educate managers and colleagues on the nuances of mental health, equipping them with the knowledge and tools needed to recognize and respond to the needs of their peers. She emphasized the importance of empathy and compassion in creating a supportive environment where everyone felt valued and understood.

As Sarah delved into the specifics of educating managers and colleagues on mental health awareness and sensitivity, she could feel the room come alive with curiosity and empathy, replaced by a sense of enlightenment and empowerment. She saw nods of understanding and heard murmurs of agreement as her colleagues embraced the idea of learning and growing together.

Together, they brainstormed ways to educate managers and colleagues on mental health awareness, from workshops and training sessions to open discussions and resource sharing.

They discussed the importance of creating a safe space for dialogue, where individuals felt comfortable asking questions and seeking guidance.

As the meeting continued, Sarah could feel a sense of enlightenment and camaraderie begin to blossom among her colleagues—a shared commitment to fostering a culture of understanding and support for mental health.

As the sun dipped below the horizon, casting a warm, golden glow over the room, Sarah knew that their journey was far from over. But armed with the knowledge and empathy they had cultivated together, she felt a sense of hope rising within her—a beacon of light to guide them through the complexities of mental health and into a future where everyone felt seen, heard, and supported.

Offering employee assistance programs (EAPs) and counseling services

"Guiding Light, Offering Solace: Providing Employee Assistance Programs"

As the day neared its end and the office embraced a tranquil atmosphere, Sarah gathered her colleagues once more, prepared to explore the indispensable role of employee assistance programs (EAPs) and counseling services—a beacon of solace in the realm of mental health support.

With a compassionate yet determined tone in her voice and a glint of reassurance in her eyes, Sarah embarked on unraveling the vital lifeline provided by EAPs and counseling services for those navigating mental health challenges. She shared stories of individuals who had found solace and strength in the guidance and assistance of counselors and support programs.

She spoke of the imperative to create a workplace where every individual felt supported and empowered to seek help when needed, knowing that they would be met with compassion and understanding. She emphasized the importance of providing access to resources that addressed the multifaceted nature of mental health, from counseling and therapy to crisis intervention and support groups.

As Sarah delved into the specifics of offering EAPs and counseling services, she could feel the room brimming with gratitude and relief, replaced by a sense of hope and reassurance. She saw nods of acknowledgment and heard murmurs of appreciation as her colleagues embraced the idea of having a safety net to rely on in times of need.

Together, they brainstormed ways to promote EAPs and counseling services in the workplace, from raising awareness through informational sessions to providing confidential access to resources. They discussed the importance of normalizing help-seeking behavior and reducing the stigma surrounding mental health.

As the meeting continued, Sarah could feel a sense of comfort and support begin to blossom among her colleagues—a shared commitment to creating a workplace where everyone felt valued and supported on their journey to well-being.

As the sun dipped below the horizon, casting a soft, comforting glow over the room, Sarah knew that their journey was far from over. But armed with the reassurance and support they had cultivated together, she felt a sense of peace rising within her—a guiding light to lead them through the darkness of mental health challenges and into a future where everyone could thrive, supported by the unwavering strength of their collective compassion.

Facilitating return-to-work programs after mental health-related absences

"Rebuilding Bridges, Embracing Renewal: Facilitating Return-to-Work Programs"

As the office settled into a quiet anticipation, Sarah once again called her colleagues together, ready to explore the transformative journey of facilitating return-to-work programs after mental health-related absences—a beacon of renewal in the realm of second chances.

With a gentle yet determined tone in her voice and a glimmer of hope in her eyes, Sarah embarked on unraveling the importance of facilitating return-to-work programs for those reintegrating into the workplace after mental health-related absences. She shared stories of individuals who had faced uncertainty and apprehension upon their return, their journeys marked by both challenges and triumphs.

She spoke of the imperative to create a supportive environment where individuals felt welcomed and valued as they resumed their professional responsibilities. She emphasized the importance of offering tailored support and accommodations to facilitate a smooth transition back to work, fostering an atmosphere of understanding and encouragement.

As Sarah delved into the specifics of facilitating return-to-work programs, she could feel the room come alive with empathy and anticipation, replaced by a sense of readiness and acceptance. She saw nods of acknowledgment and heard murmurs of encouragement as her colleagues embraced the idea of extending a helping hand to those in need.

Together, they brainstormed ways to facilitate return-to-work programs, from providing gradual reintroduction to workload to offering flexibility in scheduling and responsibilities. They discussed the importance of open communication and collaboration between managers and returning employees, ensuring that individual needs and concerns were addressed with compassion and respect.

As the meeting continued, Sarah could feel a sense of renewal and support begin to blossom among her colleagues—a shared commitment to building bridges and embracing new beginnings.

As the sun dipped below the horizon, casting a warm, golden glow over the room, Sarah knew that their journey was far from over. But armed with the compassion and determination they had cultivated together, she felt a sense of optimism rising within her—a beacon of light to guide them through the challenges of reintegration and into a future where everyone could thrive, supported by the unwavering strength of their collective empathy.

Advocating for mental health inclusivity and equality

"Champions of Change, Architects of Equality: Advocating for Mental Health Inclusivity"

As the day drew to a close and the office embraced a tranquil air, Sarah once again summoned her colleagues, prepared to embark on the transformative journey of advocating for mental health inclusivity and equality—a beacon of change in the realm of acceptance and understanding.

With a fervent yet compassionate tone in her voice and a glimmer of determination in her eyes, Sarah embarked on unraveling the imperative of advocating for mental health inclusivity and equality in the workplace. She shared stories of individuals who had faced discrimination and marginalization, their struggles amplified by a lack of recognition and acceptance.

She spoke of the urgent need to dismantle barriers and foster a culture of inclusivity and equality, where every individual felt valued and respected regardless of their mental health status. She emphasized the importance of amplifying marginalized voices and advocating for systemic change that prioritized mental health well-being.

As Sarah delved into the specifics of advocating for mental health inclusivity and equality, she could feel the room come alive with conviction and solidarity, replaced by a sense of purpose and unity. She saw heads nodding in agreement and heard murmurs of determination as her colleagues embraced the idea of becoming champions of change.

Together, they brainstormed ways to advocate for mental health inclusivity and equality, from raising awareness through advocacy campaigns to pushing for policy reforms that protected the rights of individuals with mental health conditions.

They discussed the importance of allyship and solidarity in creating a workplace where everyone felt empowered to speak up and demand justice.

As the meeting continued, Sarah could feel a sense of empowerment and hope begin to blossom among her colleagues—a shared commitment to building a future where mental health inclusivity and equality were not just ideals, but realities.

As the sun dipped below the horizon, casting a soft, ethereal glow over the room, Sarah knew that their journey was far from over. But armed with the passion and determination they had cultivated together, she felt a sense of possibility rising within her—a beacon of light to guide them through the challenges of advocacy and into a future where everyone could thrive, supported by the unwavering strength of their collective resolve.

8

Chapter 8: Leadership and Role Modeling

The role of leaders in promoting mental health in the workplace

"Guiding Lights, Inspiring Change: Leadership in Mental Health Advocacy"

As the office settled into a hushed anticipation, Sarah convened her colleagues for a pivotal discussion on leadership and its role in promoting mental health—a beacon of guidance in the realm of advocacy and support.

With a poised yet impassioned tone in her voice and a glimmer of determination in her eyes, Sarah embarked on unraveling the pivotal role of leaders in fostering a culture of mental health support within the workplace. She shared stories of leaders who had inspired change through their advocacy and compassion, their actions leaving an indelible mark on their organizations.

She spoke of the imperative for leaders to lead by example, to champion mental health initiatives and prioritize the well-being of their teams. She emphasized the importance of creating a culture where mental health was openly discussed and supported, where vulnerability was seen as a strength rather than a weakness.

As Sarah delved into the specifics of the role of leaders in promoting mental health, she could feel the room come alive with anticipation and admiration, replaced by a sense of reverence and inspiration. She saw heads nodding in agreement and heard murmurs of affirmation as her colleagues embraced the idea of leadership as a catalyst for change.

Together, they brainstormed ways for leaders to promote mental health in the workplace, from modeling healthy work-life balance to providing resources and support for mental health initiatives. They discussed the importance of fostering open communication and trust between leaders and their teams, creating an environment where everyone felt valued and supported.

As the meeting continued, Sarah could feel a sense of empowerment and hope begin to blossom among her colleagues—a shared commitment to leading with compassion and integrity in the journey toward mental health advocacy.

As the sun dipped below the horizon, casting a warm, golden glow over the room, Sarah knew that their journey was far from over. But armed with the guidance and inspiration they had cultivated together, she felt a sense of optimism rising within her—a guiding light to lead them through the challenges of leadership and into a future where mental health was embraced and celebrated as an integral part of organizational success.

Leading by example: practicing self-care and prioritizing mental wellbeing

"Walking the Talk, Nurturing the Self: Leading by Example in Mental Well-being"

As the anticipation lingered in the air, Sarah resumed her discussion with colleagues, delving deeper into the essence of leadership by example— a beacon of inspiration in the realm of self-care and mental well-being.

With a calm yet resolute tone in her voice and a glimmer of determination in her eyes, Sarah embarked on unraveling the profound impact of leading by example in nurturing one's own well-being. She shared personal anecdotes and tales of leaders who had inspired through their commitment to self-care, their actions echoing louder than words.

She spoke of the imperative for leaders to prioritize their mental well-being, to practice self-care as a means of replenishing their own reserves and setting a positive example for their teams. She emphasized the importance of creating a culture where taking time for oneself was not only accepted but encouraged, where leaders modeled healthy boundaries and resilience in the face of adversity.

As Sarah delved into the specifics of leading by example in mental well-being, she could feel the room imbued with a sense of introspection and determination, replaced by a shared resolve to prioritize self-care and mental health. She saw nods of agreement and heard murmurs of recognition as her colleagues embraced the idea of embodying the change they wished to see in their workplace.

Together, they brainstormed ways to incorporate self-care

practices into their daily routines, from mindfulness exercises to setting boundaries around work hours and responsibilities. They discussed the importance of carving out time for rest and relaxation, and the transformative power of leading with authenticity and vulnerability.

As the meeting continued, Sarah could feel a sense of empowerment and renewal begin to permeate among her colleagues—a shared commitment to nurturing their own well-being as a foundation for supporting others.

As the sun dipped below the horizon, casting a soft, comforting glow over the room, Sarah knew that their journey was far from over. But armed with the determination and self-care they had cultivated together, she felt a sense of hope rising within her—a beacon of light to guide them through the challenges of leadership and into a future where well-being was not just a priority, but a way of life.

Creating a culture of trust, transparency and empathy

"Building Bridges, Fostering Connection: Cultivating a Culture of Trust and Empathy"

As the atmosphere brimmed with anticipation, Sarah resumed the discussion, ready to delve into the transformative power of creating a culture defined by trust, transparency, and empathy—a beacon of unity in the realm of organizational dynamics.

With a gentle yet commanding tone in her voice and a glint of determination in her eyes, Sarah embarked on unraveling the profound impact of fostering a culture built on trust and empathy. She shared stories of organizations where trust and transparency had served as the bedrock of success, their teams united by a shared sense of purpose and camaraderie.

She spoke of the imperative for leaders to cultivate an environment where open communication and empathy were not just encouraged, but celebrated. She emphasized the importance of creating psychological safety, where every individual felt valued and respected, and where vulnerability was met with understanding and support.

As Sarah delved into the specifics of creating a culture of trust, transparency, and empathy, she could feel the room come alive with introspection and determination, replaced by a shared commitment to fostering connection and understanding. She saw heads nodding in agreement and heard murmurs of affirmation as her colleagues embraced the idea of building bridges and breaking down barriers.

Together, they brainstormed ways to cultivate a culture of trust, transparency, and empathy, from leading by example to fostering open dialogue and feedback. They discussed the importance of empathy in leadership, and the transformative power of understanding and supporting one another through challenges.

As the meeting continued, Sarah could feel a sense of unity and renewal begin to blossom among her colleagues—a shared commitment to building a workplace where trust and empathy flourished.

As the sun dipped below the horizon, casting a warm, golden glow over the room, Sarah knew that their journey was far from over. But armed with the determination and empathy they had cultivated together, she felt a sense of optimism rising within her—a beacon of light to guide them through the challenges of leadership and into a future where connection and understanding reigned supreme.

Communicating openly about mental health and destigmatization conversations

"Breaking the Silence, Embracing Truth: Open Dialogue on Mental Health Destigmatization"

With the anticipation palpable in the air, Sarah resumed her leadership discourse, eager to explore the transformative power of open communication surrounding mental health—a beacon of honesty in the realm of destigmatization and understanding.

With a poised yet empathetic tone in her voice and a glint of determination in her eyes, Sarah embarked on unraveling the importance of fostering open dialogue on mental health. She shared anecdotes and stories of organizations where conversations about mental health had broken down barriers and created a culture of understanding and support.

She spoke of the imperative for leaders to lead by example, to create a safe space where individuals felt empowered to share their experiences and seek support without fear of judgment or stigma. She emphasized the importance of destigmatizing mental health challenges and promoting a culture of acceptance and empathy.

As Sarah delved into the specifics of open communication about mental health, she could feel the room brimming with anticipation and empathy, replaced by a shared commitment to breaking the silence and embracing truth. She saw nods of understanding and heard murmurs of agreement as her colleagues embraced the idea of leading with vulnerability and authenticity.

Together, they brainstormed ways to foster open dialogue on mental health, from hosting town hall meetings to incorporating mental health discussions into regular team meetings. They discussed the importance of providing education and resources to empower individuals to support themselves and their peers.

As the meeting continued, Sarah could feel a sense of empowerment and solidarity begin to permeate among her colleagues—a shared commitment to fostering a workplace where everyone felt seen, heard, and supported.

As the sun dipped below the horizon, casting a soft, comforting glow over the room, Sarah knew that their journey was far from over. But armed with the honesty and empathy they had cultivated together, she felt a sense of optimism rising within her—a beacon of light to guide them through the challenges of destigmatization and into a future where mental health conversations were met with understanding and compassion.

Providing support and resources for employees

"Empowering Growth, Nurturing Resilience: Supporting Employees' Mental Health"

With the anticipation lingering in the air, Sarah continued her leadership discourse, ready to explore the pivotal role of providing support and resources for employees' mental health—a beacon of empowerment in the realm of well-being and resilience.

With a compassionate yet determined tone in her voice and a glimmer of empathy in her eyes, Sarah embarked on unraveling the transformative impact of offering support and resources for mental health. She shared stories of organizations where employees had thrived amidst challenges, their journeys marked by resilience and growth supported by accessible resources.

She spoke of the imperative for leaders to prioritize the well-being of their teams, to provide access to resources that addressed the multifaceted nature of mental health challenges. She emphasized the importance of creating a culture where seeking help was not seen as a sign of weakness, but as an act of strength and self-care.

As Sarah delved into the specifics of providing support and resources for employees, she could feel the room brimming with empathy and determination, replaced by a shared commitment to fostering resilience and well-being. She saw heads nodding in agreement and heard murmurs of affirmation as her colleagues embraced the idea of creating a safety net for those in need.

Together, they brainstormed ways to provide support and resources for employees' mental health, from offering employee assistance programs to hosting mental health workshops and providing access to counseling services. They discussed the importance of creating a supportive environment where individuals felt comfortable seeking help and accessing the resources they needed to thrive.

As the meeting continued, Sarah could feel a sense of empowerment and solidarity begin to permeate among her colleagues—a shared commitment to nurturing resilience and well-being in the workplace.

As the sun dipped below the horizon, casting a soft, comforting glow over the room, Sarah knew that their journey was far from over. But armed with the empathy and determination they had cultivated together, she felt a sense of hope rising within her—a beacon of light to guide them through the challenges of supporting mental health and into a future where every individual felt valued, supported, and empowered to thrive.

Empowering employees to take ownership of their mental health

"Empowering Independence, Cultivating Ownership: Fostering Employee Well-being"

With anticipation hanging in the air, Sarah continued her discourse, eager to explore the transformative power of empowering employees to take ownership of their mental health—a beacon of independence in the realm of well-being and self-discovery.

With a supportive yet empowering tone in her voice and a glimmer of encouragement in her eyes, Sarah embarked on unraveling the profound impact of fostering a culture where employees felt empowered to prioritize their mental health. She shared anecdotes of individuals who had embraced self-discovery and growth, their journeys marked by resilience and self-awareness.

She spoke of the imperative for leaders to create an environment where employees felt encouraged to take ownership of their mental health, to recognize their own needs and seek out resources and support when necessary. She emphasized the importance of providing tools and education to empower individuals to make informed decisions about their well-being.

As Sarah delved into the specifics of empowering employees to take ownership of their mental health, she could feel the room brimming with determination and curiosity, replaced by a shared commitment to self-discovery and growth. She saw heads nodding in agreement and heard murmurs of affirmation as her colleagues embraced the idea of fostering independence and resilience.

Together, they brainstormed ways to empower employees to take ownership of their mental health, from offering self-care workshops to providing access to online resources and support networks. They discussed the importance of creating a culture where individuals felt supported in their journey toward self-discovery and well-being.

As the meeting continued, Sarah could feel a sense of empowerment and enthusiasm begin to permeate among her colleagues—a shared commitment to fostering a workplace where every individual felt empowered to prioritize their mental health and thrive.

As the sun dipped below the horizon, casting a warm, golden glow over the room, Sarah knew that their journey was far from over. But armed with the determination and encouragement they had cultivated together, she felt a sense of optimism rising within her—a beacon of light to guide them through the challenges of empowerment and into a future where every individual felt empowered to take ownership of their mental health and live life to the fullest.

9

Chapter 9: Fostering Social Connections

The importance of social connections in workplace mental health

"Bridging Bonds, Nurturing Souls: The Power of Social Connections"

As the office buzzed with anticipation, Sarah took center stage once more, eager to explore the transformative power of fostering social connections—a beacon of unity in the realm of workplace mental health.

With a warm yet determined tone in her voice and a glint of camaraderie in her eyes, Sarah embarked on unraveling the significance of social connections in nurturing workplace mental health. She shared anecdotes and tales of camaraderie where bonds had fortified teams and uplifted spirits, their impact reverberating through the corridors of the workplace.

She spoke of the imperative for leaders to recognize the

intrinsic value of social connections, to foster an environment where individuals felt supported and valued by their peers. She emphasized the importance of creating opportunities for collaboration and connection, where laughter and camaraderie thrived alongside productivity.

As Sarah delved into the specifics of the importance of social connections, she could feel the room brimming with anticipation and enthusiasm, replaced by a shared appreciation for the power of human connection. She saw smiles of recognition and heard murmurs of agreement as her colleagues embraced the idea of fostering a sense of community and belonging.

Together, they brainstormed ways to cultivate social connections in the workplace, from team-building activities to informal gatherings and networking events. They discussed the importance of creating spaces where individuals felt comfortable reaching out to one another, fostering a culture of support and camaraderie.

As the meeting continued, Sarah could feel a sense of unity and excitement begin to permeate among her colleagues—a shared commitment to fostering social connections and nurturing workplace well-being.

As the sun dipped below the horizon, casting a soft, comforting glow over the room, Sarah knew that their journey was far from over. But armed with the camaraderie and enthusiasm they had cultivated together, she felt a sense of optimism rising within her—a beacon of light to guide them through the challenges of fostering social connections and into a future where every individual felt supported, valued, and connected.

Building strong team relationships and camaraderie

"Weaving Unity, Strengthening Bonds: Building Team Camaraderie"

With the energy of anticipation swirling around the room, Sarah continued her discourse, eager to explore the transformative potential of building strong team relationships and camaraderie—a beacon of unity in the realm of workplace cohesion.

With a spirited yet grounded tone in her voice and a glint of unity in her eyes, Sarah embarked on unraveling the profound impact of fostering strong team relationships and camaraderie. She shared anecdotes of teams who had transcended challenges through their unwavering support for one another, their bonds of camaraderie becoming the bedrock of success.

She spoke of the imperative for leaders to cultivate an environment where teams felt united and connected, where collaboration and camaraderie thrived. She emphasized the importance of creating opportunities for team members to get to know each other on a personal level, fostering trust and empathy in the process.

As Sarah delved into the specifics of building strong team relationships and camaraderie, she could feel the room brimming with enthusiasm and solidarity, replaced by a shared determination to strengthen bonds and forge connections. She saw nods of agreement and heard murmurs of affirmation as her colleagues embraced the idea of fostering a sense of belonging and unity.

Together, they brainstormed ways to cultivate strong team relationships and camaraderie, from team-building exercises to regular check-ins and social outings. They discussed the importance of creating a supportive environment where team members felt valued and respected, and where differences were celebrated as strengths.

As the meeting continued, Sarah could feel a sense of excitement and unity begin to permeate among her colleagues—a shared commitment to building a workplace where teams felt connected and empowered to achieve greatness together.

As the sun dipped below the horizon, casting a warm, golden glow over the room, Sarah knew that their journey was far from over. But armed with the unity and determination they had cultivated together, she felt a sense of optimism rising within her—a beacon of light to guide them through the challenges of building camaraderie and into a future where every team felt like a family, united in purpose and bound by mutual respect and support.

Encouraging social activities and team-building exercises

"Fostering Fun, Strengthening Bonds: Embracing Social Activities"

As the excitement lingered in the air, Sarah continued her exploration, eager to unveil the transformative power of encouraging social activities and team-building exercises—a beacon of unity in the realm of workplace engagement.

With a lively yet grounded tone in her voice and a spark of enthusiasm in her eyes, Sarah embarked on unraveling the profound impact of embracing social activities and team-building exercises. She shared anecdotes of teams who had forged lasting connections through shared experiences, their bonds growing stronger with each laughter-filled moment.

She spoke of the imperative for leaders to create opportunities for teams to come together outside of work, to engage in activities that fostered camaraderie and strengthened bonds. She emphasized the importance of creating a culture where fun and laughter were celebrated alongside hard work and dedication.

As Sarah delved into the specifics of encouraging social activities and team-building exercises, she could feel the room brimming with excitement and anticipation, replaced by a shared eagerness to embrace new experiences and forge connections. She saw smiles of anticipation and heard murmurs of agreement as her colleagues embraced the idea of infusing joy and camaraderie into their workplace culture.

Together, they brainstormed ideas for social activities and team-building exercises, from outdoor adventures to game nights and volunteering opportunities. They discussed the importance of creating a diverse range of experiences that catered to different interests and preferences, fostering inclusivity and unity among team members.

As the meeting continued, Sarah could feel a sense of anticipation and camaraderie begin to permeate among her colleagues—a shared commitment to building a workplace where relationships thrived and connections were cherished.

As the sun dipped below the horizon, casting a warm, golden glow over the room, Sarah knew that their journey was far from over. But armed with the excitement and camaraderie they had cultivated together, she felt a sense of optimism rising within her—a beacon of light to guide them through the challenges of fostering social connections and into a future where every team felt united, supported, and uplifted by the power of shared experiences.

Facilitating peer support networks and mentorship programs

"Strength in Numbers, Wisdom in Guidance: Nurturing Peer Support and Mentorship"

As the anticipation swirled in the air, Sarah delved deeper into the exploration, eager to unveil the transformative potential of facilitating peer support networks and mentorship programs— a beacon of solidarity and guidance in the realm of workplace relationships.

With a compassionate yet determined tone in her voice and a glimmer of solidarity in her eyes, Sarah embarked on unraveling the profound impact of fostering peer support networks and mentorship programs. She shared anecdotes of individuals who had found strength and guidance through the support of their peers, their journeys enriched by the wisdom and experience of mentors.

She spoke of the imperative for leaders to create opportunities for employees to connect with one another on a deeper level, to seek guidance and support from those who have walked similar paths. She emphasized the importance of fostering a culture where individuals felt empowered to share their challenges and successes, and where mentorship was seen as a reciprocal relationship built on trust and mutual respect.

As Sarah delved into the specifics of facilitating peer support networks and mentorship programs, she could feel the room brimming with empathy and enthusiasm, replaced by a shared commitment to fostering connections and growth. She saw nods of understanding and heard murmurs of agreement as her colleagues embraced the idea of nurturing relationships that transcended hierarchy and fostered collaboration.

Together, they brainstormed ideas for peer support networks and mentorship programs, from informal buddy systems to structured mentoring initiatives. They discussed the importance of creating spaces where individuals felt comfortable seeking guidance and support, and where mentors could offer insight and encouragement to help others thrive.

As the meeting continued, Sarah could feel a sense of solidarity and empowerment begin to permeate among her colleagues—a shared commitment to fostering a workplace where everyone felt supported and uplifted by the strength of their connections.

As the sun dipped below the horizon, casting a soft, comforting glow over the room, Sarah knew that their journey was far from over. But armed with the solidarity and guidance they had cultivated together, she felt a sense of optimism rising within her—a beacon of light to guide them through the challenges of fostering peer support networks and mentorship programs and into a future where every individual felt empowered to grow and succeed, supported by the wisdom and compassion of their peers.

Addressing isolation and loneliness in remote or virtual work environments

"Bridging Distances, Embracing Connection: Combatting Isolation in Remote Work"

As the discussion unfolded, Sarah delved deeper into the exploration, eager to unveil strategies for addressing isolation and loneliness in remote or virtual work environments—a beacon of connection in the realm of distance and separation.

With a compassionate yet resolute tone in her voice and a glimmer of empathy in her eyes, Sarah embarked on unraveling the profound impact of combatting isolation and loneliness. She shared anecdotes of individuals who had grappled with the challenges of remote work, their journeys marked by moments of disconnection and longing for community.

She spoke of the imperative for leaders to recognize the unique challenges of remote work and to create opportunities for virtual connection and support. She emphasized the importance of fostering a sense of belonging and inclusion, even in the absence of physical proximity.

As Sarah delved into the specifics of addressing isolation and loneliness in remote work environments, she could feel the room brimming with empathy and determination, replaced by a shared commitment to fostering connection and support. She saw nods of understanding and heard murmurs of agreement as her colleagues embraced the idea of bridging distances and creating virtual communities.

Together, they brainstormed ideas for combatting isolation and loneliness in remote work, from virtual coffee chats to online team-building exercises and support groups. They discussed the importance of creating spaces where individuals could share their experiences and seek support from one another, fostering a sense of camaraderie and belonging.

As the meeting continued, Sarah could feel a sense of solidarity and resilience begin to permeate among her colleagues—a shared commitment to overcoming the challenges of remote work and fostering connection in the face of distance.

As the sun dipped below the horizon, casting a warm, golden glow over the room, Sarah knew that their journey was far from over. But armed with the empathy and determination they had cultivated together, she felt a sense of optimism rising within her—a beacon of light to guide them through the challenges of combatting isolation and loneliness and into a future where every individual felt connected, supported, and valued, no matter the distance.

Celebrating achievements and milestones as a team

"Honoring Milestones, Sharing Triumphs: The Joy of Collective Achievement"

As the discussion continued, Sarah ventured further into the exploration, eager to unveil the transformative power of celebrating achievements and milestones as a team—a beacon of camaraderie in the realm of shared success.

With a jubilant yet grounded tone in her voice and a glimmer of excitement in her eyes, Sarah embarked on unraveling the profound impact of honoring milestones and sharing triumphs. She shared anecdotes of teams who had come together to celebrate their successes, their bonds strengthened by moments of collective achievement.

She spoke of the imperative for leaders to create opportunities for teams to celebrate their victories, both big and small. She emphasized the importance of fostering a culture where accomplishments were recognized and celebrated, fueling motivation and strengthening bonds.

As Sarah delved into the specifics of celebrating achievements and milestones as a team, she could feel the room brimming with anticipation and enthusiasm, replaced by a shared sense of pride and camaraderie. She saw smiles of excitement and heard cheers of encouragement as her colleagues embraced the idea of coming together to celebrate their successes.

Together, they brainstormed ideas for celebrating achievements and milestones, from virtual celebrations to in-person gatherings and team outings. They discussed the importance of creating traditions and rituals that honored the hard work and dedication of each team member, fostering a sense of unity and accomplishment.

As the meeting continued, Sarah could feel a sense of joy and unity begin to permeate among her colleagues—a shared commitment to celebrating their victories and supporting one another in their journey toward success.

As the sun dipped below the horizon, casting a warm, golden glow over the room, Sarah knew that their journey was far from over. But armed with the excitement and camaraderie they had cultivated together, she felt a sense of optimism rising within her—a beacon of light to guide them through the challenges of fostering social connections and into a future where every achievement was met with celebration and every milestone was shared with pride and joy.

10

Chapter 10: Creating a Culture of Wellbeing

Defining a culture of wellbeing and its components

"Nurturing Wellness, Building Prosperity: Crafting a Culture of Wellbeing"

As anticipation filled the room, Sarah began to explore the essence of creating a culture of wellbeing—a beacon of harmony in the realm of workplace prosperity.

With a serene yet determined tone in her voice and a glimmer of inspiration in her eyes, Sarah embarked on unraveling the multifaceted nature of a culture of wellbeing. She shared stories of organizations where every aspect of the workplace was designed to promote health and happiness, their environments fostering growth and fulfillment.

She spoke of the imperative for leaders to define and prioritize a culture of wellbeing, to cultivate an environment where every individual felt supported and empowered to thrive. She emphasized the importance of recognizing the interconnectedness of physical, mental, and emotional health, and the role that each component played in fostering overall wellbeing.

As Sarah delved into the specifics of defining a culture of wellbeing and its components, she could feel the room brimming with curiosity and determination, replaced by a shared commitment to nurturing wellness and prosperity. She saw heads nodding in agreement and heard murmurs of affirmation as her colleagues embraced the idea of creating a workplace where every individual felt valued and supported in their journey toward holistic health.

Together, they brainstormed ideas for cultivating a culture of wellbeing, from offering wellness programs to promoting work-life balance and fostering a supportive environment for mental health. They discussed the importance of leadership buy-in and employee engagement in driving cultural change, and the transformative power of small actions in creating a ripple effect of positivity and wellbeing.

As the meeting continued, Sarah could feel a sense of optimism and unity begin to permeate among her colleagues—a shared commitment to crafting a workplace where wellness was not just a priority, but a way of life.

As the sun dipped below the horizon, casting a soft, comforting glow over the room, Sarah knew that their journey was far from over. But armed with the determination and inspiration they had cultivated together, she felt a sense of hope rising within her—a beacon of light to guide them through the challenges of creating a culture of wellbeing and into a future where every individual felt supported, empowered, and fulfilled in their pursuit of happiness and health.

Aligning organizational values with mental health initiatives

"Harmony in Purpose, Unity in Action: Aligning Values with Mental Health Initiatives"

As the conversation progressed, Sarah delved deeper into the essence of aligning organizational values with mental health initiatives—a beacon of coherence in the realm of workplace harmony.

With a poised yet impassioned tone in her voice and a glimmer of conviction in her eyes, Sarah embarked on unraveling the transformative potential of aligning values with mental health initiatives. She shared stories of organizations where every decision and action reflected a commitment to prioritizing the wellbeing of their employees, their values serving as a guiding light in times of uncertainty.

She spoke of the imperative for leaders to ensure that organizational values were not just words on a page, but principles that were lived and breathed every day. She emphasized the importance of aligning mental health initiatives with these values, ensuring that they were integrated into every aspect of the workplace culture.

As Sarah delved into the specifics of aligning organizational values with mental health initiatives, she could feel the room brimming with determination and purpose, replaced by a shared commitment to authenticity and integrity. She saw nods of agreement and heard murmurs of affirmation as her colleagues embraced the idea of aligning their actions with their values, even in the face of challenges.

Together, they brainstormed ideas for integrating mental health initiatives into the fabric of the organization, from incorporating wellbeing into performance metrics to fostering a culture of open communication and support. They discussed the importance of leading by example and empowering employees to take ownership of their mental health, creating a workplace where everyone felt valued and supported.

As the meeting continued, Sarah could feel a sense of unity and clarity begin to permeate among her colleagues—a shared commitment to aligning their values with their actions and creating a culture where wellbeing was a priority.

As the sun dipped below the horizon, casting a warm, golden glow over the room, Sarah knew that their journey was far from over. But armed with the determination and unity they had cultivated together, she felt a sense of purpose rising within her—a beacon of light to guide them through the challenges of aligning values with mental health initiatives and into a future where every decision and action reflected a commitment to the wellbeing of their employees.

Integrating mental health into company policies, benefits, and programs

"Integrating Care, Cultivating Support: Enriching Policies, Benefits, and Programs"

With anticipation lingering in the air, Sarah ventured further into the exploration, eager to unveil the transformative potential of integrating mental health into company policies, benefits, and programs—a beacon of compassion in the realm of workplace support.

With a compassionate yet resolute tone in her voice and a glimmer of empathy in her eyes, Sarah embarked on unraveling the profound impact of enriching policies, benefits, and programs with a focus on mental health. She shared anecdotes of organizations where employees felt supported and valued, their wellbeing prioritized through comprehensive policies and benefits.

She spoke of the imperative for leaders to ensure that mental health was integrated into every aspect of the workplace, from hiring and onboarding to performance management and employee development. She emphasized the importance of creating a culture where mental health support was accessible and stigma-free, empowering employees to prioritize their wellbeing.

As Sarah delved into the specifics of integrating mental health into company policies, benefits, and programs, she could feel the room brimming with empathy and determination, replaced by a shared commitment to nurturing support and care. She saw heads nodding in agreement and heard murmurs of affirmation as her colleagues embraced the idea of creating a workplace where every individual felt valued and supported in their mental health journey.

Together, they brainstormed ideas for enriching company

policies, benefits, and programs with a focus on mental health, from offering flexible work arrangements to providing access to counseling services and mental health resources. They discussed the importance of training managers and employees on mental health awareness and creating a culture where seeking help was encouraged and supported.

As the meeting continued, Sarah could feel a sense of solidarity and empowerment begin to permeate among her colleagues—a shared commitment to integrating mental health into every aspect of the workplace and creating a culture where every individual felt valued, supported, and empowered to thrive.

As the sun dipped below the horizon, casting a soft, comforting glow over the room, Sarah knew that their journey was far from over. But armed with the empathy and determination they had cultivated together, she felt a sense of optimism rising within her—a beacon of light to guide them through the challenges of integrating mental health into company policies, benefits, and programs and into a future where every individual felt supported and valued in their mental health journey.

Promoting work-life integration and flexibility

"Harmony in Motion, Flexibility in Balance: Nurturing Work-Life Integration"

As the discussion continued, Sarah ventured deeper into the exploration, eager to unveil the transformative potential of promoting work-life integration and flexibility—a beacon of harmony in the realm of personal and professional balance.

With a tranquil yet determined tone in her voice and a glimmer of balance in her eyes, Sarah embarked on unraveling the profound impact of nurturing work-life integration. She shared anecdotes of organizations where employees felt empowered to prioritize both their personal and professional lives, their productivity and satisfaction flourishing as a result.

She spoke of the imperative for leaders to create an environment where work-life balance was not just encouraged, but actively promoted. She emphasized the importance of offering flexibility in work arrangements, empowering employees to design schedules that met their individual needs and responsibilities.

As Sarah delved into the specifics of promoting work-life integration and flexibility, she could feel the room brimming with anticipation and enthusiasm, replaced by a shared commitment to nurturing wellbeing and fulfillment. She saw smiles of recognition and heard murmurs of agreement as her colleagues embraced the idea of creating a workplace where individuals could thrive both professionally and personally.

Together, they brainstormed ideas for promoting work-life integration and flexibility, from offering remote work options to implementing flexible hours and paid time off policies. They discussed the importance of setting boundaries and creating a culture where taking breaks and prioritizing self-care were celebrated as essential components of success.

As the meeting continued, Sarah could feel a sense of harmony and empowerment begin to permeate among her colleagues—a shared commitment to promoting work-life integration and flexibility and creating a workplace where every individual felt supported and valued in their pursuit of balance.

As the sun dipped below the horizon, casting a warm, golden glow over the room, Sarah knew that their journey was far from over. But armed with the tranquility and determination they had cultivated together, she felt a sense of peace rising within her—a beacon of light to guide them through the challenges of promoting work-life integration and flexibility and into a future where every individual could thrive, both professionally and personally, in harmony with their true selves.

Investing in employee development and growth opportunities

"Nurturing Growth, Cultivating Potential: Investing in Employee Development"

As the conversation flowed, Sarah delved deeper into the exploration, eager to unveil the transformative potential of investing in employee development and growth opportunities—a beacon of empowerment in the realm of personal and professional advancement.

With a determined yet nurturing tone in her voice and a glimmer of ambition in her eyes, Sarah embarked on unraveling the profound impact of nurturing growth and development. She shared anecdotes of organizations where employees were encouraged to pursue their passions and expand their skill sets, their confidence and engagement soaring as they embraced new challenges.

She spoke of the imperative for leaders to invest in employee development, to create opportunities for learning and growth that aligned with both individual aspirations and organizational goals. She emphasized the importance of fostering a culture where curiosity and innovation were celebrated, and where every individual felt supported in their journey toward success.

As Sarah delved into the specifics of investing in employee development and growth opportunities, she could feel the room brimming with ambition and excitement, replaced by a shared commitment to nurturing talent and potential. She saw heads nodding in agreement and heard whispers of enthusiasm as her colleagues embraced the idea of creating a workplace where every individual could thrive and excel.

Together, they brainstormed ideas for investing in employee development and growth opportunities, from offering training and mentorship programs to providing tuition assistance and opportunities for career advancement. They discussed the importance of creating a culture where continuous learning and improvement were valued and where every individual felt empowered to pursue their goals and aspirations.

As the meeting continued, Sarah could feel a sense of empowerment and possibility begin to permeate among her colleagues—a shared commitment to investing in employee development and growth opportunities and creating a workplace where every individual could reach their full potential.

As the sun dipped below the horizon, casting a warm, golden glow over the room, Sarah knew that their journey was far from over. But armed with the determination and ambition they had cultivated together, she felt a sense of excitement rising within her—a beacon of light to guide them through the challenges of investing in employee development and growth opportunities and into a future where every individual could thrive and succeed, empowered by the support and opportunities they received.

Measuring and evaluating the impact of mental health initiatives on organizational outcomes

"Evaluating Progress, Honoring Impact: Measuring the Success of Mental Health Initiatives"

As the dialogue progressed, Sarah delved into the final frontier of their exploration, eager to unveil the transformative potential of measuring and evaluating the impact of mental health initiatives on organizational outcomes—a beacon of accountability in the realm of progress and growth.

With a determined yet reflective tone in her voice and a glimmer of accountability in her eyes, Sarah embarked on unraveling the profound impact of assessing the effectiveness of mental health initiatives. She shared anecdotes of organizations where data-driven insights were used to refine and enhance support systems, their dedication to continual improvement driving positive change.

She spoke of the imperative for leaders to embrace metrics and evaluation tools that could quantify the impact of mental health initiatives on organizational outcomes. She emphasized the importance of transparency and accountability in fostering a culture where feedback and learning were valued, and where success was measured not just by numbers, but by the tangible impact on employee wellbeing and performance.

As Sarah delved into the specifics of measuring and evaluating the impact of mental health initiatives, she could feel the room brimming with contemplation and determination, replaced by a shared commitment to accountability and progress. She saw heads nodding in agreement and heard murmurs of recognition as her colleagues embraced the idea of using data to inform decision-making and drive positive change.

Together, they brainstormed ideas for assessing the effectiveness of mental health initiatives, from conducting employee surveys to tracking key performance indicators related to wellbeing and engagement. They discussed the importance of creating a culture where feedback was welcomed and acted upon, and where leaders were held accountable for the impact of their actions on employee health and happiness.

As the meeting drew to a close, Sarah could feel a sense of clarity and purpose begin to permeate among her colleagues—a shared commitment to measuring progress and honoring the impact of their efforts on organizational outcomes.

As the sun dipped below the horizon, casting a soft, comforting glow over the room, Sarah knew that their journey was far from over. But armed with the determination and accountability they had cultivated together, she felt a sense of assurance rising within her—a beacon of light to guide them through the challenges of measuring and evaluating the impact of mental health initiatives and into a future where every decision and action was driven by a commitment to the wellbeing and success of their employees.

About the Author

Goodson Mumba is a multifaceted individual known for his diverse expertise and prolific contributions across various fields. As an infopreneur, thought leader, and spiritual leader, he has inspired countless individuals through his insightful teachings and impactful writings. Mumba is also an accomplished author, with several notable works to his name, including "Understanding Corporate Worship," "The Years I Spent in a Week," "Management By Harmony," "The CEO's Diary," "Change to Change" and "Creative Thinking for results" His literary works span topics ranging from business management to personal development and spirituality, reflecting his broad range of interests and insights.

With a Master of Business Leadership (MBL) and a Bachelor of Arts in Theology (BTh), Mumba brings a unique blend of business acumen and spiritual wisdom to his work. His educational background is further enriched by a Group Diploma in Management Studies, providing him with a solid foundation in organizational dynamics and leadership principles. Additionally, Mumba holds diplomas in Education Psychology,

Leadership and Management Styles, Organizational Behaviour, Financial Accounting, Economic Growth and Development, and Project Management, showcasing his commitment to continuous learning and professional development.

Mumba's expertise extends beyond traditional academic disciplines, encompassing areas such as Neuro-Linguistic Programming (NLP) and Positive Psychology. His diverse skill set is complemented by a range of certifications, including Creative Problem Solving and Decision Making, Life Coaching Fundamentals and Techniques, Professional Life Coaching, and Performance Management System Design. These certifications reflect Mumba's dedication to equipping himself with the tools and knowledge necessary to empower others and drive positive change.

As an author, Mumba's writings reflect his deep understanding of human nature, organizational dynamics, and spiritual principles. His works offer practical insights, actionable strategies, and inspirational guidance for individuals seeking personal growth, professional success, and spiritual fulfillment. Mumba's holistic approach to life and leadership resonates with readers worldwide, making him a respected figure in both the business and spiritual communities.

Overall, Goodson Mumba's diverse background, extensive knowledge, and profound insights make him a sought-after speaker, mentor, and author. His commitment to excellence, lifelong learning, and service to others continues to inspire individuals to unlock their full potential and lead lives of purpose and significance.

Goodson Mumba is renowned for initiating the concept of Management by Harmony, revolutionizing traditional management practices with a focus on balanced and holistic approaches. He has authored two influential books on this subject: "Introduction to Management by Harmony" and its sequel, "Management by Harmony."

Mumba's work has significantly impacted the field, offering innovative strategies for fostering organizational harmony and efficiency. His contributions continue to shape contemporary management theories and practices.